The Impressionists

Denis Thomas

The Impressionists

CASTLE BOOKS

Frontispiece
The bridge at Argenteuil *detail*
see plate 24

Published in the USA by Castle Books
Distributed to the trade in the USA by
Book Sales Inc.
110 Enterprise Avenue, Secaucus, New Jersey

© Copyright 1975 The Hamlyn Publishing Group Limited
London · New York · Sydney · Toronto
Astronaut House, Feltham, Middlesex, England

ISBN 0-89009-006-8
Library of Congress catalogue card number 74-80970

Printed in Czechoslovakia
51689

Plate 1
Edouard Manet (1832–83)
Monet in his studio boat
1874
oil on canvas
32½ × 39¼ in (83 × 100 cm)
Neue Pinakothek, Munich

Contents

Manet and the beginnings of Impressionism

In art, as in all human activity, revolutions are both necessary and inevitable. The Impressionist revolution was no exception. It was necessary if painting in Europe was to break away from the postures of institutional classical and Romantic art; and it was inevitable because, midway through the nineteenth century, the men and the motivation were at hand. Like other revolutionaries before them, they were a band of individuals, widely different in character and background. They were neither of one class nor of one mind. None of them particularly relished a life of poverty and ridicule. A few were protected against starvation by family resources. Others knew hunger, borrowed from friends to keep going, or scratched a living on the edge of the commercial world. Between them they produced work which in the space of twenty years helped to change not only the course of Western painting but also the nature of the artist's relationship to his subject, his materials and himself.

Since history insists on dates, the year 1874 stands as the opening of the great Impressionist epoch. In April of that year a group of young French artists who shared, in varying degrees, a feeling of rejection by the art Establishment of the day, held a group exhibition in Paris. Among them were Claude Monet, Auguste Renoir, Camille Pissarro, Paul Cézanne, Edgar Degas and Alfred Sisley. An older painter, Eugène Boudin, joined them out of comradeship. The only woman in the group, Berthe Morisot, braved the risk of antagonising the Salon, where her work was readily accepted, to exhibit with her friends. With another of their circle, Armand Guillaumin, they numbered eight out of a total of thirty exhibitors, most of whose names are now forgotten. The exhibition, held in a vacant photographer's studio on the corner of the Boulevard des Capucines, was given a long-winded title suggestive of many hours' fruitless argument: 'Société Anonyme des Artistes Peintres, Sculpteurs, Graveurs, etc.' However, among the paintings on view was one which was destined to give the exhibition a name which would stick. It was by Claude Monet, and it was called *Impression : sunrise* (plate 2).

The reception which the exhibition was given seems, in retrospect, hysterically hostile. The gibes of the critics and cartoonists (one of them showed a policeman preventing a pregnant woman from entering the exhibition for fear of injury to her unborn child) fell indiscrimi-

Plate 2 (see also plate 26)
Claude Monet (1840–1926)
Impression: sunrise *detail*
1872
oil on canvas
$19\frac{1}{2} \times 24\frac{1}{2}$ in (50 × 62 cm)
Musée Marmottan, Paris

The painting which gave the Impressionists their name was of the sun seen through the sea-mist at Le Havre, where Monet was living in 1872. When it was shown in 1874 in the first group exhibition (they then called themselves the Société Anonyme des Artistes Peintres) it was singled out for sarcastic reference by the critic of *Le Charivari*, Louis Leroy, who secured for himself an unexpected immortality by flinging the word 'Impressionist' in the exhibitors' faces. A hundred years later the novelty and daring sketchiness are still apparent. It is not, perhaps, the most subtle work of which Monet was capable, nor is it altogether characteristic of his style and technique at that stage in his career. It remains, for all that, one of the seminal paintings of its time.

Plate 3
Armand Guillaumin (1841–1927)
The Bridge of Louis Philippe, Paris
1875, oil on canvas, 18 × 23¾ in (45 × 60 cm)
National Gallery of Art, Washington
(Chester Dale Collection)

Though not among the great figures of the Impressionist period, Guillaumin was a talented member of the group and shared their struggles in the early years. A neighbour and friend of Cézanne, he had been a student at the Académie Suisse with Pissarro, through whose efforts both he and Cézanne were invited to show at the first Impressionist exhibition. Guillaumin might well have developed into an original artist of some note, but he was relieved of the need to paint for a living by winning 100,000 francs in the state lottery. He continued to paint throughout a long life, and became the last survivor of the 1874 exhibitors, outliving Monet by one year.

nately on the band of painters now dubbed, scoffingly, 'Impressionists'. Amid the uproar, they recognised in that name the description they had been looking for; until then they had regarded themselves primarily as 'realists', taking as their subject-matter the everyday life around them and depicting it on the spot, in deliberately unacademic terms which caught the pace and style of the streets and cafés and the suburban pleasure grounds where they felt at home. Renoir, for one, seized on the new name. It would tell the public exactly what the new painters were up to: 'Here is the kind of painting you won't like. If you come in, so much the worse for you— you won't get your money back!'

In the ensuing hundred years the impact of Impressionist painting on men's minds, and on their minds' eyes, has been such as to leave only the vaguest images to compare it with. In that sudden blaze of light most other painting of the time seems shadowy and dim. The

Impressionists were contemptuous of most of it, though they respected their immediate forbears such as Delacroix, Courbet and Corot, all of whom influenced them to some degree and whose names are as lustrous as theirs, in the end, became. But there is no doubt that the kind of paintings exhibited each year at the Paris Salon, and against which the Impressionists rebelled, were of an almost unrelieved mediocrity. The Salon was both the arbiter and the image of public taste and the only means by which an aspiring painter could find patrons and win recognition. Since the middle of the seventeenth century it had enjoyed a prestige unrivalled in Europe. Starting as an exhibition reserved exclusively for members of the French Academy, the pet of French royalty and the aristocracy, it had burgeoned into a supposedly democratic institution to which any painter might submit his work. His chance of being accepted depended on the propriety of his subject-matter and the seemliness of his technique. He would

Plate 4
Armand Guillaumin (1841–1927)
The Seine at Charenton
1878
oil on canvas
23½ × 39½ in (60 × 100 cm)
Louvre, Paris

Guillaumin here achieves the distinctively Impressionist suffusion of light in a subject introducing some of the group's favourite passages: summery sky, glinting water, industrial shapes flanked by red-roofed houses, and a pervasive sense of open-air enjoyment.

Plate 5
Edouard Manet (1832–83)
Le déjeuner sur l'herbe
1862–63
oil on canvas
$83\frac{3}{4} \times 106\frac{1}{4}$ in (214 × 270 cm)
Louvre, Paris

With this painting Manet announced the emancipation of the artist from the academic conventions of his time. It is based on a classical original, Giorgione's *Fête champêtre*, which as a student he had copied in the Louvre, and on Raphael's drawing of *The judgement of Paris*. Manet had long been interested in interpreting this subject in terms of natural light and atmosphere, and it was the realism of his treatment which so shocked visitors to the Salon des Refusés when it was shown in 1863. Manet's models were Victorine Meurent, who also posed as the equally scandalous *Olympia* (plate 6), his brother-in-law Ferdinand Leenhoff, and his brother Eugène. The mixture of styles–fresh, natural still-life in the foreground, harsh studio lighting on the group of figures, and the conventionally idyllic passage in the background– disconcerted Manet's contemporaries. The *Déjeuner* is one of those rare paintings which mark a decisive turning point in Western art. Almost overnight, Manet found himself the leader of the band of young painters who came to be known as Impressionists.

be judged by a jury dominated by functionaries and bureaucrats and presided over by an Academician. Gallery after gallery was hung, two or three lines deep, with the work of painters who felt no urge to step out of line. Crowds came to stroll and gossip and compare prices. Ingres, a revered Establishment painter, called it 'a bazaar in which the tremendous number of objects is overwhelming, and business rules instead of art'. The exhibitors who commanded the biggest crowds, and prices, in the Impressionists' lifetime were painters such as Jean Louis Meissonier, who specialised in genre and battle scenes executed in finicking detail; Jean-Léon Gérôme, a sugary Neo-Classicist whose total non-comprehension of Impressionist painting (he called it 'filth') did not, surprisingly enough, deter the young Maillol and Vuillard from becoming his pupils; and Alexandre Cabanel, showered with honours in his lifetime and virtually forgotten ever since, except perhaps as the painter of a voluptuous *Birth of Venus* which Napoleon III bought from the Salon of 1863, the year of a seminal event in the development of modern art, the Salon des Refusés.

That spring, the Salon jury rejected over three thousand of the five thousand paintings submitted. No doubt a majority of these were feeble or incompetent by any standard, but the sweeping dismissal of so many artists' work caused an outcry. There was, in effect, nowhere else for an ambitious artist to exhibit. Painters who held one-man shows at dealers' galleries were suspect. Manet had just taken the risk of showing a group of his paintings with a dealer called Martinet, which must have prejudiced his chances with the gentlemen of the Salon. For less daring spirits the Salon was all; rejection amounted to public censure from which there was no redress. The affronted *refusés* sent up a howl of complaint, with the press in support. The hubbub reached the ears of Louis Napoleon, who liked on occasion to simulate a liberality not often evident in his political actions. The Emperor made an unannounced visit to the Salon and declared that most of the rejected paintings might be hung after all, if only so that the public could make up their own minds. He ordered that any of the rejected artists who chose to do so could have their work hung, separately from the Salon, in the adjoining Palais de l'Industrie.

Manet, with three paintings, was among those who took up the challenge. So were Pissarro, also with three, Whistler and Cézanne, with one each. Two of Manet's canvases were exercises in his neo-Velazquez manner. The other was a painting destined to immortalise the Salon des Refusés, as this part of the exhibition was promptly called, and to make Manet's name notorious. The crowds who flocked to see what the fuss was about found themselves confronted by a painting of two young men picnicking in a wooded glade with a pair of female companions, one of whom, stark naked, gazed out of the canvas with an air of mild curiosity (plate 5). The artist had

Plate 5 **Le déjeuner sur l'herbe**

called it *Le bain*, later to be changed to *Le déjeuner sur l'herbe*, but soon
it was being called other names. 'A practical joke, a shameless sore,'
protested one critic. 'An absurd composition,' said another. An
English art pundit, P. J. Hamerton, complained that 'some wretched
Frenchman' had brutalised a classic theme, adding that 'the nude,
when painted by vulgar men, is inevitably indecent'. The Emperor
himself agreed, and reportedly struck at Manet's painting with his
cane.

   To a public brought up to expect a picture to tell a story, or point
a moral, or at the very least to leave the spectator in no doubt what it
was about, the *Déjeuner* was a shock. There were no clues to the
artist's intentions. Perhaps he never had any. The painting was just
a painting, then? And of course they were, to that extent, right in

Plate 6
Edouard Manet (1832–83)
Olympia
1863
oil on canvas
51 × 74¾ in (130 × 190 cm)
Louvre, Paris

Painted in the same year as the *Déjeuner sur l'herbe*, Manet's *Olympia* achieved a similar sensation at the Salon of 1865. Manet regarded it as his masterpiece, a view shared by many of his friends and supporters. Cézanne (plate 57) and Gauguin later painted their own versions of it. The cryptic title was not Manet's, but was suggested by his friend Zacharie Astruc just before the painting was taken to the Salon. Manet's main source was the *Venus of Urbino* of Titian, in the Uffizi, which he saw on his second visit to Italy in 1856, but there are equally obvious similarities to Goya's *Maja nude* in the Prado. The painting was regarded as indecent in subject and insultingly crude in execution: the exact opposite of Manet's character and intentions. Baudelaire, a close companion, wrote: 'Manet, whom people think wild and insane, is simply a very straightforward, unaffected person, as reasonable as can be, but unfortunately touched by romanticism from birth.' In 1871 Manet valued the *Olympia* at 20,000 francs, but when it came up for sale a year after his death it failed to reach even half that figure. Eventually Monet organised a private fund to buy the painting for the French nation. It has hung in the Louvre since 1907.

their judgement. The classical references on which Manet had drawn, notably Giorgione's *Fête champêtre* in the Louvre, only added to the critics' exasperation. Their reactions to a work which, a century later, is recognisably of our own age, shows how deep was the gulf between what was expected of painters in Manet's time and what he felt to be the true function of the artist. He knew there was an important fight to be won, and he saw the real battlefield as the Salon. 'My worst enemies are forced to look at my pictures there,' he said. On the other hand, he was genuinely taken aback at the hostile reception to the *Déjeuner*. He did not see himself as the object of scandal and was distressed to find himself cast in the role of a publicity-seeker saboteur. He regarded himself as a serious painter using methods learned or adapted from his studies of the masters. If his work didn't come out like theirs, it was because his motives were different, not because he was less of an artist.

Manet was far from being a stereotype of the revolutionary painter. By birth and education he belonged to the French upper middle class, and he made no effort to dress, talk or behave otherwise. He was distinguished by an ironic detachment which enabled him to stand back from the involvements which agonised many of his friends, and which from the beginning gave his work a penetrating realism. At the time of *Le déjeuner sur l'herbe* he was still favourably regarded in polite artistic society. True, the first picture he ever submitted to the Salon, the *Absinthe drinker* in 1859, had been rejected; but two years later two of his pictures (a portrait of his parents and *The guitarist*) had been accepted. *The guitarist* even won him an honourable mention. In the years that followed, during the gradually accelerating Impressionist revolution, Manet was frequently accepted at the Salon—a circumstance which seems to set him apart from Pissarro, Monet, Cézanne and Sisley, who were carrying on the struggle at a different level. But then, it is the historians who have cast Manet as the leader of the Impressionist movement. He himself had no such pretensions. He belongs with Degas, two years his junior and a kindred spirit in some ways, who used to deny he was an Impressionist at all. And yet Manet's example inspired and encouraged his young contemporaries, especially Monet, Renoir and Sisley, who became known as *la bande à Manet* – Manet's gang. Until Manet suddenly emerged as the most adventurous painter of the age, these young painters had looked to Courbet for their example: Courbet, the archetypal Romantic painter, belligerent, extrovert, a fervent radical rich in battle honours from skirmishes with the authorities. In the year of the Salon des Refusés, Courbet was forty-four and Manet thirty-one. Of the other Impressionists-to-be, Pissarro was a year older than Manet, Renoir was twenty-two, Monet twenty-three and Sisley twenty-four. After the sensations of the Salon des Refusés, Courbet retreated into middle age and Manet became the automatic leader-figure of the young avant-garde.

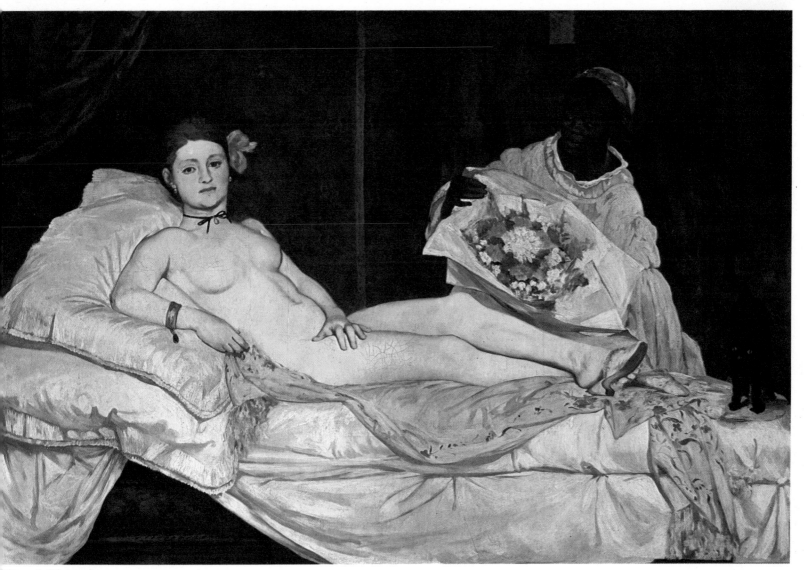

Plate 6 **Olympia**

Tactfully, or perhaps strategically, Manet submitted for the next
year's Salon two paintings of a kind less likely to agitate the jury than
the now notorious *Déjeuner*: a dead Christ and a bullfight subject.
Nevertheless his treatment of the figure of Christ was hotly attacked
for its departures from traditional iconography, and the pair of
attendant angels for looking more like winged *midinettes* than celes-
tial beings. Here Manet's realism worked against him, and he committed an almost wilful liberty in depicting the wound in Christ's
side on the left instead of the right. Though the characteristically
impersonal mood stamps the painting with Manet's intelligence, he
soon abandoned religious subjects.

Having, in a sense, recovered some credit at the Salon, Manet was
ready for his next *coup d'éclat*. On his easel was a finished painting
which, had he chosen to follow up the *Déjeuner* with a similar gesture
in the next year's Salon, might well have been rejected. (He saw the
Salon des Refusés as a once-for-all sensation, not to be repeated.)
Manet held back this new painting for the Salon of 1865, perhaps

13

Plate 7
Edouard Manet (1832–83)
Portrait of Emile Zola
1867–68
oil on canvas
57 × 43½ in (190 × 110 cm)
Louvre, Paris

Zola, a school-friend of Cézanne and a staunch
supporter of the Impressionists through his
critical writings, was quick to defend Manet in
the years when he was being most bitterly
attacked. He wrote: 'Our fathers laughed at
M. Courbet, and now we go into raptures over
him. We laugh at M. Manet, and our sons will
go into raptures over his canvases. A place
awaits M. Manet in the Louvre.' The Louvre is
where Manet's portrait of Zola now hangs. It
contains many elements relevant to the Impressionists' world: a Japanese screen, an Utamaro
print, a small version of the *Olympia* and a glimpse
of a print by Goya after Velasquez. The magazine
in which Zola came to Manet's defence is on the
table, with the artist's name on the cover. The
painting is both a portrait and a tribute.

reckoning that by then the jury would be beginning to reconcile themselves to his more adventurous work.

It was a portrait of a young woman lying on a bed, dressed only in
a bracelet, earrings and a neckband, her left hand spread over her
mons veneris, in an attitude borrowed from Poussin's *Triumph of
Flora* in the Louvre. Beyond the bed was a negress bearing a bouquet
in a paper wrapping. On the end of the bed a black cat arched its
back. Manet called it *Olympia* (plate 6), perhaps in vague acknowl-
edgement of its classical antecedents, which included Titian and Goya
as well as Poussin, though a more generally accepted explanation is
that it was so named by a friend, the poet Zacharie Astruc, just before
being delivered to the Salon. As in the *Déjeuner*, the naked young
woman seems deliberately painted to involve the spectator, with a
gaze of such worldly unconcern as to be sexually shocking. Manet
knew it was his masterpiece.

It was accepted at the Salon. Perhaps Manet's impeccable artistic
sources persuaded a majority of the jury to see it, despite its startling
modernity, as belonging in the main stream of European painting.
One likes to think that they responded, in spite of their prejudices,
to the stunning mastery of the design, in which colours of infinite
delicacy are brutally brought up against blacks and near-blacks, the
tones abutting against each other with no gradations, the shadows
forced back by the light falling on the bed and flesh. Not since the
unequivocal nudes of Cranach, 350 years earlier, had a female body
been painted with quite such candour. Above all, that self-possessed
little face with its incurious gaze has for a hundred years defied men to
walk past without returning a glance. Olympia's presence is as spell-
binding as one of Baudelaire's women (he was a close friend of Manet)
in whom the poet sees 'a fusion of candour and wantonness . . . Her
arms, her legs, her thighs and her loins glistening as if polished with
oil.'

All this, however, meant nothing to the critics. They were horrified
by the blatant nudity, the realism, and the assault on the spectator's
senses. Some of them recoiled from the painting as if from a dead
body, and indeed found corpse-like characteristics in Manet's treatment of the flesh. Théophile Gautier, a distinguished man of letters,
wrote: '*Olympia* can be understood from no point of view, even if
you take it for what it is, a puny model stretched out on a sheet. The
colour of the flesh is dirty, the modelling non-existent. The shadows
are indicated by more or less large smears of blacking. What is to be
said of the negress . . . or for the black cat which leaves its ugly foot-
prints on the bed? We would still forgive the ugliness, were it only
truthful . . . The least beautiful woman has bones, muscles, skin, and
some sort of colour.' Courbet remarked, objectively enough: 'It's
flat, it isn't modelled; like the Queen of Spades on a playing card just
out of her bath.' After the critics came the crowds. *Olympia* was the
only picture they wanted to see. Two guards were posted in front of

it to prevent disturbances; and after a couple of days it was moved to a high, inconspicuous position on another wall.

With two extraordinary paintings in the space of as many years, Manet had announced the arrival of modern art. What distinguished these works from anything else to be seen in Paris at that time was the sheer painterly quality of Manet's mind and hand. Instead of disguising his arts, as had been the convention among painters for as long as anyone could remember, he blatantly emphasised them. In a painting by Manet the spectator joined in the action. His surfaces were not simulations of real textures: they were unmistakably paint laid on canvas. He was demonstrating that, for the painter, reality consists in attacking his canvas. It may seem a commonplace a century later; in Manet's time it was a heresy. To disregard perspective, modelling, shading from dark into light—this was an affront to the accepted canons of painting and an insult to all pedagogues. The

Plate 8
Edouard Manet (1832–83)
Engagement of the Kearsarge and the Alabama
1864
oil on canvas
$52\frac{3}{4} \times 50$ in (134×127 cm)
John G. Johnson Collection, Philadelphia

On a summer day in 1864, people watching from the coast at Cherbourg were witnesses of a battle between the Confederate privateer *Alabama* and the Union corvette *Kearsarge*, which had waited offshore to engage the *Alabama* as she put out from the harbour after refuelling. Manet's response to the drama was to join the crowd of sightseers who went out in small boats for a closer view, which accounts for the unconventional angle from which he reconstructed the event for this painting. Characteristically, Manet reports the action without rhetoric.

Plate 9
Edouard Manet (1832–83)
The Seine at Argenteuil
1874
oil on canvas
24½ × 40½ in (62 × 103 cm)
The Dowager Lady Aberconway Collection,
London

The Impressionists were attracted to the river
scenery outside Paris for both artistic and
economic reasons: they found the light, colour
and activity stimulating, and in any case they
were mostly too hard up to live in the city.
Manet's family owned a property not far from
Argenteuil, on the Seine, and he was a frequent
visitor. Monet first went there in 1871, to be
joined by Renoir and Sisley. Like these members
of the group, Manet painted on the river and

notion of art as make-believe, or as an experience in which the spectator can allow his mind to penetrate beyond the painter's superficial
intention—this too was challenged by Manet's insistence that the
viewer should take him literally, compelling him to see the marks he
had made on the canvas as well as what those marks stood for. The
two great paintings in which he made these intentions plain are
revolutionary works of art.

Though Manet's detractors continued to heap insults on his work,
a small group of defenders gave him enthusiastic support. Astruc and
Baudelaire, and Emile Zola, (whose vehement pro-Manet article
in the review *L'Evénement* got him the sack) were all active propa-
gandists in his cause. With *la bande à Manet* they became a sort of
brotherhood, talking and planning at their favourite meeting place,
the Café Guerbois in the Avenue de Clichy. 'Let's go and see Manet,'

Plate 10 **Venice, the Grand Canal** *see page 18*

Pissarro would tell the others, 'he will stand up for us.' Manet, with his air of slightly dandified distinction, assumed leadership of the group, and embarked on a prolific ten years of painting and drawing which embraced portraits, flower studies, scenes at the races—anything appropriate to his well-known credo: 'Paint what you see—instantly.' When the Union corvette *Kearsage* engaged the Confederate gun-boat *Alabama* off Cherbourg, he recorded the event with a characteristic sense of drama by going out in a small boat for a closer look. His painting of the action (plate 8) is very different from the conventional heroic composition; it is more like a hurried snapshot, and the more convincing for being viewed from eye-level, with the expanse of sea cramming the subject into the upper third of the picture. In similar response to a news event he painted the execution of the Archduke Maximilian, who after seizing power in Mexico with

along the banks, capturing the sense of liberation and enjoyment which drew the crowds from Paris at weekends. *The Seine at Argenteuil*, while characteristically individual in style, is typical of Manet's response to the aims and enthusiasms of his Impressionist friends of the 1870s.

Plate 10
Edouard Manet (1832–83)
Venice, the Grand Canal
1874
oil on canvas
$18\frac{3}{4} \times 22\frac{1}{2}$ in (48 × 57 cm)
Shelburne Museum, Vermont

Even without one or other of the young Impressionists at his side, Manet was happy to embrace the Impressionist palette and method, as in this painting from a visit to Venice in 1874. Venice, which has been the undoing of many a good painter with its dissolving shapes and magical light, inspired Manet to this dazzling exercise in form and colour. The treatment of the water, in strokes of pure colour, is typically Impressionist, and so is the deliberately blurred background. On the other hand, Manet never abandoned his characteristic use of black, outlawed by the other members of the group. Here it is used to give impact and presence to the central object in the composition, the gondola.

Plate 11
Edouard Manet (1832–83)
La servante de bocks
The beer waitress
1878–79
oil on canvas
$38\frac{1}{4} \times 30\frac{1}{2}$ in (98 × 77 cm)
National Gallery, London

'That Manet,' complained Degas, 'as soon as I did dancers, he did them.' The charge is unjust, but Degas was not a particularly magnanimous friend. The café-concerts of Paris were favourite meeting places of the Impressionists, who delighted in the atmosphere, noise and bustle of people enjoying themselves. This painting was originally part of a larger one which was cut in two and later reworked by the artist. It retains the spontaneity of an original sketch while conforming to Manet's instinctive feeling for forms, however awkwardly Nature arranges them. As usual in his work the outlines are solid and firm and the modelling is suggested by strong contrasts of light and colour. In a version of this subject in the Louvre the grey derby is replaced by a top hat, and the whole composition is cropped more closely around the central group, accentuating the almost cinematic effect of movement and drama.

the help of French troops was promptly left to his fate by Louis Napoleon when the United States protested. Manet, to show his disgust at this betrayal, dressed the firing squad in French uniforms. His debt to Goya's masterpiece, the *Third of May*, is obvious; but there is a uniquely Manet-like touch in the attitude of the soldier who, standing apart from the death-dealing group, cocks his rifle with professional calm.

By occasionally using another painter's composition as a starting point for his own, Manet laid himself open to charges of plagiarism. Degas, whose support of Manet was by no means single-minded, said in later years that Manet 'could never do anything but imitate' (though he was also to say, 'We never knew how great he was' – a handsome admission from an equal). Manet's use of well-known masterpieces to reinforce his personal response to people, scenes and events can be seen as a means of forcing the viewer to accept the rightness of what he was doing. These painterly quotations have an almost scriptural power, carrying with them the authority of unchallengeable truth.

In what sense, then, can Manet be called an Impressionist painter? In spite of working closely with the Impressionist group and sharing their broad aims, Manet remained very much an individualist. He never abandoned the Salon, and envied the fashionable painters whose work brought them honours and rewards far beyond any which came his way. In a stylistic sense, too, Manet's early work, including the *Déjeuner* and *Olympia*, has nothing in common with what Pissarro, Renoir, Sisley and the rest were doing at the time. He favoured dark backgrounds and sombre blacks, as in the paintings of Velazquez, whom he discovered in the Louvre early in his career. The Impressionists set out by rejecting black from their palettes altogether; to them, shadows were made up of the surrounding tones, never casting sharp lines, softening gradually into lighter shapes.

For all that, they learned from Manet, and Manet learned from them. Though he was a conspicuous absentee from the first Impressionist Exhibition in 1874, in that same year he was painting at Argenteuil on the Seine (plate 9) with Monet, who was living there, and Renoir. Several of Manet's paintings of about this time show an Impressionist influence: a lighter, sunnier palette, stippled brushwork, and the distinctive Impressionist sense of airiness. His response to Venice, late in 1874, was markedly Impressionistic (plate 10), and in *Chez le père Lathuile*, dated 1879, he achieved a fusion of his lifelong attitude to portraiture and the quick, glancing technique of Impressionism as exemplified in similar subjects by Renoir and Monet. By then he had only four years left, in which he moved back to his own personal style in a series of dazzling paintings centred on the Parisian demi-world of bars, circuses, courtesans and night clubs. In 1883, after an operation to amputate a gangrenous leg, in agony and delirium, he died. He was fifty-two.

Plate 11 **La servante de bocks**

Plate 12 **Self-portrait**

Edgar Degas

Of Manet's circle the closest to him in age, intellect and temperament was Edgar Degas, whom Manet first met in 1859, the year of his first rejection from the Salon. The two men shared similar social backgrounds: Degas' grandfather had founded a bank and there was plenty of money in the family. He was born in 1834, one of a family of five, to the Creole wife of De Gas *père* (Edgar subsequently spelled his name in the less pretentious form, Degas). His family wanted him to become a lawyer (so had Manet's, offering him the French navy as a second-best) but he seems to have had little difficulty in getting himself enrolled at the Ecole des Beaux Arts to study under a former pupil of Ingres. He soon became bored with classwork and repetitive copying in the Louvre, and at the age of twenty-two took himself off to Italy to study the masters. Back in Paris he took a studio on the Left Bank and began painting historical subjects. So far he showed no signs of joining the artistic 'underground'; practically the only signs of a response to real events were to be seen in his paintings of the theatre and ballet, a lifelong enthusiasm.

Then came his meeting with Manet. Their talents were of similar kinds, each aiming at directness and simplicity at the expense of finish and detail: the opposite of the grandiose picture-making expected of professional painters. Degas sympathised entirely with Manet's impatience with all that was superfluous in a painting. Conciseness, said Manet, was both necessary and elegant: 'The verbose painters are bores.' Degas found Manet's famous detachment much to his taste, and adopted the same stance in his own work. Again like Manet, Degas was essentially a townee. He was more at home in the city streets and salons than in the country fields where the Barbizon painters and their heirs found both inspiration and style; and he had an instinctive distaste for the extrovert gestures of Courbet and the Romantic-Realist school which briefly flourished in the glare of his celebrity. He was quite shocked at Manet's respect for official honours. When Manet once recommended him to accept an award, he rounded on him with, 'This isn't the first time I've realised what a bourgeois you are, Manet!' The ambivalent nature of their relationship might also have had something to do with their conflicting political attitudes. Manet, despite his respect for the apparatus of social power, was a convinced republican. Degas was unashamedly a snob. Again, though

Plate 12
Edgar Degas (1834–1917)
Self-portrait
1854–55
oil on canvas
$31\frac{3}{4} \times 26$ in (81 × 64 cm)
Louvre, Paris

Degas' withdrawn and somewhat enigmatic character is indicated in his self-portraits. Mary Cassatt, who understood him perhaps better than anybody, called him 'a pessimist', adding: 'He dissolves you . . .'

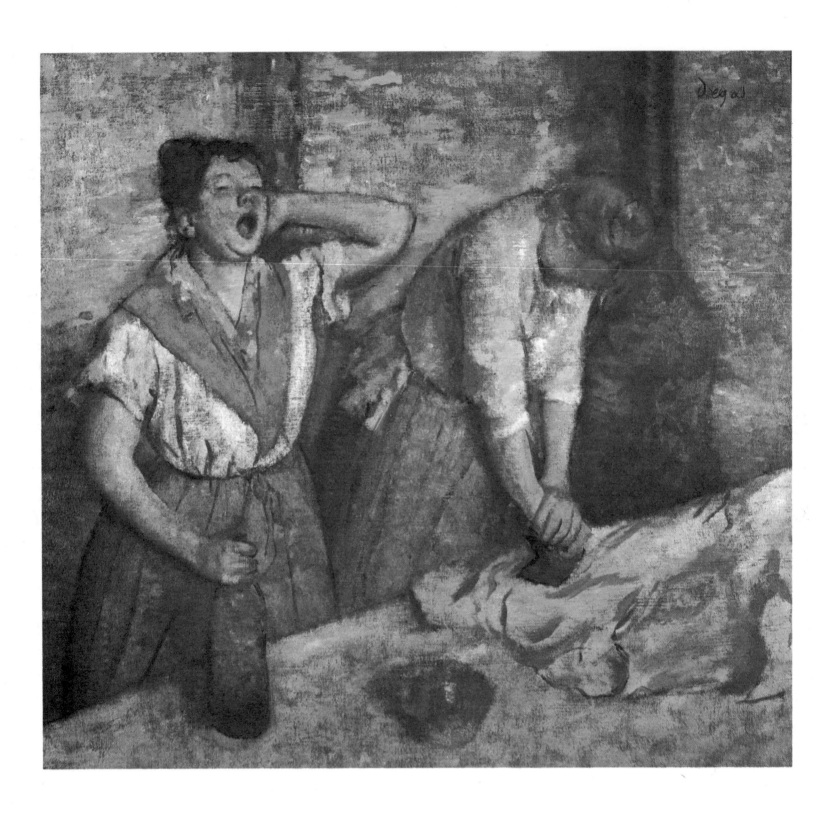

Plate 13
Edgar Degas (1834–1917)
Women ironing
about 1884
oil on canvas
30 × 31¾ in (76 × 81 cm)
Louvre, Paris

Degas shared the Impressionists' interest in the humbler aspects of everyday life as subjects for painting, and as a consummate figure draughtsman he produced works which, like this one, catch actions and movements at their most expressive. The left-hand laundress's yawn of fatigue, and her accompanying gesture, lend additional force to the two-handed downward thrust of her companion. Also typical of Degas is the absence of ingratiation in his treatment of the two working women. 'Art,' he said, 'cannot be done with the intention of pleasing.'

Plate 14
Edgar Degas (1834–1917)
At the seaside
about 1876
oil thinned with turpentine on paper
18½ × 32½ in (47 × 82 cm)
National Gallery, London

Though Degas had less in common with the Impressionists than his close association with them might suggest, he grew to share their belief in the kind of realism which comes of a fleeting glance that captures the whole. This French seaside scene has similarities to the work of Manet at this period, but it also contains strong elements of draughtsmanship and design which are present in nearly all his work. The woman having her hair combed is a motif which recurs in later paintings.

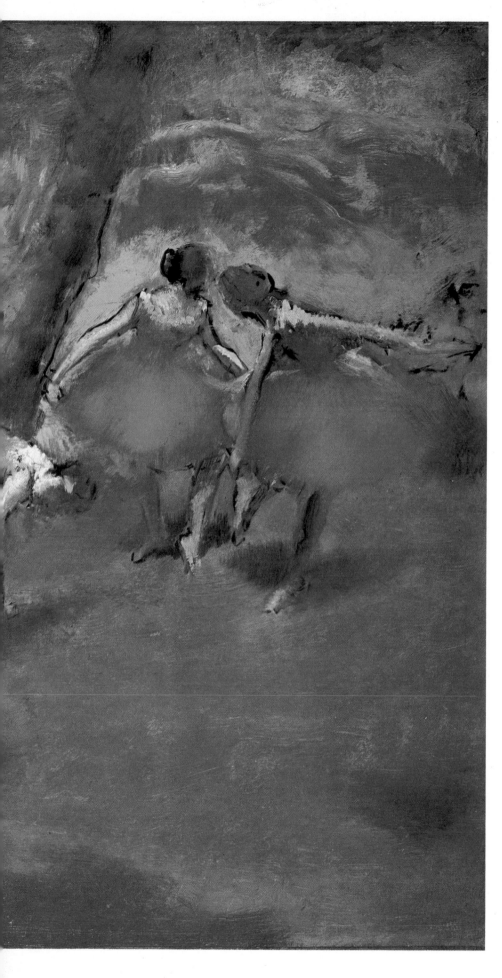

Plate 15
Edgar Degas (1834–1917)
Before the performance
about 1896–98
oil on canvas
$18\frac{3}{4} \times 24\frac{3}{4}$ in (47 × 62 cm)
National Gallery of Scotland, Edinburgh

'Everyone has talent at twenty-five,' said Degas, 'the difficulty is to have it at fifty.' He was fifty when he painted this characteristic study of a *corps de ballet* taking their positions before the curtain rises. Degas was fascinated by the theatre, and not least by the lights and garish colours which briefly glamorised the young dancers. He said: 'The intriguing thing is not to show the source of the light but the effects of the lighting.'

Plate 16
Edgar Degas (1834–1917)
The morning bath
1883
pastel
27¾ × 17 in (70 × 43 cm)
Art Institute of Chicago

Degas was obsessed with drawing, which he said was 'not form, but a way of seeing form . . . You must go over the same subject ten times, a hundred times. In art nothing must appear accidental, even a movement.' His studies of women, their private attitudes and gestures, are miracles of drawing. When he turned from oils to pastel owing to failing sight, and made himself a master of the medium, he produced some of the finest studies of the nude since antiquity. Until then, as he said, the nude had always been represented in poses which presupposed an audience. 'But these women of mine, simple creatures, are uninterested in any concerns than those involved in their physical condition . . . It's as if one were looking at them through a key-hole.'

they shared so much that was important to them as painters, their methods of work were different. Manet believed in putting down what he saw first time. 'If you've got it, that's it.' Degas, on the other hand, said: 'There's nothing less spontaneous than my art.' The brilliant naturalism which he seemed to achieve so easily was the result of deliberation and hard work.

In great artists, human qualities have a way of enlarging themselves through their work, and so it is with Degas. Whatever his public self might have seemed, his private self, the artist, was capable of dignity and compassion surpassing that of moralising painters such as Millet and, in England, the Victorians. In a Degas study of a shopgirl or a laundress or a singer in a café there is an unsentimental tenderness which makes us look and look again (plate 13). Like Manet, he does not paint types; he paints real people. In his own life he did not make room for love, or even close friendship, explaining: 'There is love and there is work, and we have only one heart.'

His work did not unduly antagonise the jury at the Salon where he exhibited regularly after 1865. In 1870 came the war with Prussia, scattering the band of friends. Degas sailed to the United States, an experience which excited him (he wrote home about it like any tourist) and which produced at least one portrait, of Estelle, the blind wife of his brother René, which ranks among his masterpieces. She sits with her arms folded protectively across her pregnant body, looking into an endless distance. Another work from this period, *The Cotton Exchange*, is as carelessly arranged as a press photograph and with just that kind of immediacy. It shows his uncle's office in New Orleans, and the figures are portraits of the family and staff. Degas seemed to revel in the new possibilities opened up by photography. He delighted in painting from unconventional angles as if perched on a chair, and in the ruthless way in which the lens chops off shapes for which there is no room. Ironically, in view of his obvious attraction to photographic techniques, Degas was suffering from an eye ailment which partially obscured his vision. One thinks of him squinting through an imaginary viewfinder, allowing the composition to assume its involuntary form. He even bought a camera, and used it for organising his pictures.

Back in Paris things had changed. The Opéra had been burned down, depriving Degas of one of his major pleasures and sources of ideas. But most of the young painters he admired were still there, thinking about holding a group exhibition. Degas joined them. It was as if, after his absence, his mind was clear about what he should do next. By joining the insurgents he was turning his back on a career within the established professional structure. He ran the same risks as they did, of ridicule and rejection; and he was not, like most of them, hardened in the fire. He was not an easy companion, and had little taste for the bohemian hurly-burly in which they lived. But he gave them his support, and under their influence his own work became

Plate 16 **The morning bath**

perceptibly higher-keyed, with the bright colours and shimmering lightness of touch which distinguish Impressionist painting at this, its historical high-water mark.

Degas joined the Impressionists in all but one of their exhibitions; but meanwhile his own fortunes suffered a severe blow. The family's finances were found to be in such a tangle after the death of his father that Degas, to save the family from bankruptcy, sold his own substantial collection of pictures, only to find that his brother René, husband of Estelle (whom he afterwards abandoned), was likewise in dire straits following some unlucky speculations on the stock market. Degas and a brother-in-law each paid half of what was owing, which effectively reduced Degas to a financial state not much different from that of his painter friends. Now dependant on selling his paintings for a living, Degas began to produce work which, while uncompromisingly his own, compelled the public to enjoy it.

To these years belong the sketches and paintings of the ballet, in which Degas' enthusiasm and craftmanship combine so successfully that no major painter has ever again dared to take the ballet as his theme (plate 15). He grew steadily more successful and respected. As he did so he withdrew from the world. His sight continued to trouble him; and when he found he could no longer manage oils to his satisfaction he turned to a new medium, pastel. Somehow, thanks to a special fixative known only to himself, he transformed pastel into a medium hardly less subtle than watercolour. Instead of his colours turning each other muddy as one was laid over another, Degas was able to achieve miracles of lightness and delicacy which have never been equalled in the medium. He had always been a skilled draughtsman; now, with a crayon in his hand, he became a master. The pleasure these drawings gave, and give still, establishes him among the greatest draughtsmen of modern times. In them he passes beyond the fixed image of the photograph to suggest the next movement, and the one after that, in a single stroke. The dancer's body becomes an instrument, which in her inactive moments she checks and tunes like a violinist.

No one has captured the private moments of a woman, unobserved, absorbed in some female ritual, with such piercing curiosity (plate 16). To the end Degas retained that essential quality of detachment which he shares with Manet. Other artists, treating such subjects, might become *voyeurs*. Degas does not react sensually to what he sees and draws; on the contrary, he seems disinterested in the conventional attitudes of coquetry and desire. This gives his figures of women infinitely more interest and, perhaps contrary to his own intentions, an unexpected pathos. It is typical of Degas that he could produce works which give such pleasure without in any way involving himself with the spectator.

'Drawing,' he said, 'is not what one sees but what others have to be made to see.' This is in accord with his belief that art is a sleight of

Plate 17 **Café-concert at the Ambassadeurs**

Plate 18 **The absinthe drinkers**

hand by means of which a painter can deceive the spectator into accepting the device as the reality. This brings him nearer to pre-Impressionist attitudes to art than he would perhaps have cared to admit, and certainly it seems a contradiction of Manet's dictum that painting should always look like painting, whatever subject the artist sets himself. But there are many contradictions in Degas, both in his work and his opinions. For instance, he acknowledged the part that a painter's unconscious self plays in helping him create works of art. Only when the artist no longer knows what he is doing, Degas said, does he do good things. Many of his later works are of this kind; the marvellously gifted practitioner, working at the same familiar subjects over and over again until they become second nature, can every so often let his unconscious, poetic self come through. Such moments brought him close to abstract painting, when as an old man, his sight—like Monet's—grew weak and unreliable, he painted less what he saw than what he felt to be true.

Degas occupies his own place in the history of European painting, regardless of his association with the men who called themselves Impressionists. He refused to be lumped together with them even in the years when he was closest to them, helping to organise their exhibitions and showing his own work alongside theirs. He was essentially a non-joiner, and nearly everything that is known about his private relationships suggests that he was a difficult and sometimes cruel friend. But his artistic kinship with the Impressionists is real enough. Like them, he took his subjects from the streets and bars and entertainments of Paris, without sharing their delight in parks and riverside greenery, farmland and village landscapes (plate 17). Like Manet, and like Renoir, he made the human figure the centre of much of his work and marked his human subjects with his own signature. He shared with the others an informality of pose and subject which makes his work easy to receive and enjoy. While Manet could say, and demonstrate, that a painter's job is immediately to put down what he sees, Degas insisted that there is nothing natural about a painting. It requires, he said, 'as much cunning, as much malice, and as much vice as committing a crime'. He was nevertheless an Impressionist in a technical sense: an artist more concerned with the light in which subjects and movements exist than in the substance. His fascination with light can be seen in the way he uses it to dissolve outlines, as of dancers' dresses, and the distinction he makes between natural brightness and the glare of artificial light. Though he never painted from nature—his open-air subjects were worked up from sketches—there is no hint of studio stuffiness in anything he did.

His last years were pitiable. In 1908 his sight failed and he was forced to give up work altogether. He had never made close friends, nor had he ever married. Old, nearly blind, rich, revered and alone, he lived on in Paris, shuffling about the streets with no one to visit and nowhere to go. At last, on 27th September, 1917, he died.

Plate 18
Edgar Degas (1834–1917)
The absinthe drinkers
about 1877
oil on canvas
$36\frac{1}{4} \times 26\frac{3}{4}$ in (92 × 67 cm)
Louvre, Paris

This famous painting, a portrait study of the actress Ellen Andrée and the painter-etcher Marcellin Desboutin, has been interpreted as a study in dissipation. Degas certainly had no such intention; he was no moralist, and believed in painting people's portraits in what he called 'familiar and typical attitudes'. The actress and the artist, habitués of the same cafés as *la bande à Manet*, are set down with an honesty which has nothing to do either with sympathy or censure. This, one feels, is exactly how they were.

Plate 19 **The jetty at Deauville**

Plate 20 **Windmills in Holland**

Claude Monet

Claude Monet, destined to be regarded as the quintessential Impressionist, owed a lifelong debt to a painter whose work, distinguished as it is, stands outside the Impressionist achievement: Eugène Boudin. When Monet met Boudin at the age of fifteen he was on the brink of becoming a commercial artist. Born in Paris, he had spent his boyhood in Le Havre, where his father was a grocer and ship chandler. The young Monet exhibited his drawings of local scenes in the window of a local stationer and picture-framer, and it was there that Boudin, who himself found ample subject-matter along the quays and beaches of his native Normandy, noticed Monet's work. He offered advice, and invitations to accompany him on painting excursions. Monet was not much interested to begin with, but suddenly, as he explained in later life, it was 'as if a veil had been removed. The mere example of this artist, devoted to his art and his independent way of life, made me realise what painting could mean.' More specifically, Boudin showed Monet the subtleties of sunlight and water, and the pleasures of painting out of doors (plate 19). His parents looked askance at Boudin as a master for their talented son, who was sent instead to Paris to study under the teacher Thomas Couture. Unlike Manet, who spent six years with Couture before finally breaking away, Monet stayed hardly any time at all. He then enrolled at the Académie Suisse, a more free-spirited institution on the Quai des Orfèvres. He met Pissarro there, an association which was to have fruitful consequences for both young men. But before he could make much progress he was called up for military service and shipped off to North Africa.

The experience did him no harm; on the contrary, he declared himself delighted with the light and colour of Algeria. After two years he succumbed to the climate and was sent home. Boudin, who continued to take an interest in him, introduced him to the brilliant young Dutch painter Jongkind, with whom he found aims and ideas in common (plate 20). Already Monet was committed to landscape painting. Returning to Paris in 1862 he quickly made friends with Renoir, Sisley and Bazille, and the four of them practised their shared interest in out-of-doors landscape by painting in the forest of Fontainebleau. He did not please his parents by associating with these nobodies, and when he refused to enter the prestigious Ecole des Beaux Arts, as they wished, they cut his allowance. In the 1865 Salon, the year of Manet's notori-

Plate 19
Eugène Boudin (1824–98)
The jetty at Deauville
1869
oil on canvas
$9 \times 12\frac{1}{2}$ in (23×32 cm)
Louvre, Paris

Boudin's paintings of harbour and beach scenes along the Normandy coast, with their luminous, colours, animated groups of figures and melting lights, had a direct effect on the young Monet, whom he befriended in his teens. Boudin, already modestly established as a painter, gave his support to the first Impressionist exhibition in 1874 but never exhibited with the group again. Following, as he called it, 'my own little road, however untrodden it might be,' he led a contented enough life away from the upheavals of Paris. Like Corot, and like the Impressionists, he painted outdoors. 'Everything painted directly and on the spot,' he said, 'has a force and liveliness which one never recaptures in the studio.'

Plate 20
Johan Barthold Jongkind (1819–91)
Windmills in Holland
watercolour
$10\frac{1}{4} \times 17\frac{3}{4}$ in (26×45 cm)
Fogg Art Museum, Harvard University, Cambridge, Massachusetts (Grenville L. Winthrop Bequest)

Jongkind was a Dutchman who did much of his best work in France, particularly in Normandy where he painted with Boudin. He in turn introduced Monet to Jongkind, whose oils and watercolours of this period have all the qualities which the Impressionists most admired. That he did not join their company was due to recurrent bouts of alcoholism, compounded by psychological stress. Jongkind died in the asylum at Grenoble, acknowledged by discerning critics as the painter most worthy to be called the true initiator of Impressionism.

Plate 21
Claude Monet (1840–1926)
La Grenouillère
1869
oil on canvas
29¼ × 39¼ in (74 × 100 cm)
Metropolitan Museum of Art, New York
(Bequest of Mrs H. O. Havemeyer, 1929. The
H. O. Havemeyer Collection)

At Bougival on the Seine there was a popular
boating and bathing place known as La Grenouillère (the Frog-pool). Here the young Monet and
his friend Renoir painted together in 1869,
sometimes in styles so similar that Renoir remarked in later years that he could not always
tell his own work of that date from Monet's. It
could be said that Impressionism was set on its

ous *Olympia*, Monet (their names were confused then, as they sometimes are today) showed two seapieces which one critic declared were
the best marine paintings in the exhibition. In that year, too, he met the
young girl, Camille Doncieux, who became his model and his mistress.
In a mounting chaos of poverty and debt, and with Camille pregnant,
he burned two hundred of his paintings rather than have them seized
by creditors. Then, leaving Camille in Paris, he took refuge with an
aunt near Le Havre. From there he bombarded his friends with re-
quests for money, and they responded as best they could.

In April 1869 Boudin visited him, and reported to a friend that
Monet was 'completely starved, his wings clipped'. The two paintings
he had submitted to the Salon had been refused, but he was taking his
revenge, Boudin said, by exhibiting at a Paris paint merchants, Le-

Plate 22 **The beach at Trouville** *see page 36*

touche, a study of the beach at Sainte-Adresse 'which has horrified his fellow artists'. Boudin added: 'There is a crowd outside the window all the time, and for the young people the generalisation of this picture has produced fanatical responses.' Meanwhile Camille had had her baby, Bazille standing as godfather. In June 1870 Monet married her and took her to Trouville, where he painted a carefree beach scene (plate 22). That same summer the war with Prussia started. Monet fled to England to avoid military service.

He was away for only a year, but his stay in London proved to be one of the formative influences in his career. The mists and melting hues of a northerly landscape were no less suited to Impressionism than the clear, ringing colours of the south (plate 23). Monet's views of London scenes rank among his most sensitive and successful works

true path in those few weeks of creative partnership. Monet and Renoir now proved to themselves the validity of their notion that there is no black in shadows, only variants of the surrounding tones, and that the real colour of an object is the colour of the light, or lights, in which we see it. This, combined with short brushstrokes laying dabs of unmixed colours one against another, became the distinguishing marks of what was to come. Renoir's version of this subject can be seen in plate 42.

Plate 22
Claude Monet (1840–1926)
The beach at Trouville
1870
oil on canvas
$14\frac{3}{4} \times 18$ in (37×45 cm)
National Gallery, London

In the summer of 1870 Monet was just thirty.
Newly married to his mistress, Camille Doncieux,
who had just had a baby, he spent a few weeks at
the seaside resort of Trouville, a favourite
sketching ground of the friendly Boudin. There
on the beach, holding his canvas on his knee, he
painted Camille and her sister in flat, broad
strokes, grains of sand spattering the paint as he
worked. In July, war broke out between France
and Prussia, and within a few weeks Monet had
crossed to England, leaving Camille and the
child behind. The tensions of that summer find
no echo in *The beach at Trouville*, in which
youthful confidence is matched with skills learned
from Boudin and Manet. But he never painted a
picture like this again.

Plate 23
Claude Monet (1840–1926)
The Thames below Westminster
1871
oil on canvas
$18\frac{1}{2} \times 28$ in (47×72 cm)
National Gallery, London

Monet, self-exiled in London during the Franco-
Prussian war, found the mists and hazy outlines
of a more northerly landscape no less sympathetic
as subject-matter than the summery hues of
France. With Camille Pissarro, who joined him
in London, he set about painting with enthusiasm.

Plate 24
Claude Monet (1840–1926)
The bridge at Argenteuil
1874
oil on canvas
$23\frac{1}{2} \times 31\frac{1}{2}$ in (60×80 cm)
Louvre, Paris

In a marvellously creative burst of energy at
Argenteuil in the summer of 1874, Monet produced a series of paintings of the river and its
pleasure craft which have no parallel until the
waterlily sequence of his old age. Here the light
takes charge of everything: tones, distances,
shapes, composition. The colours, applied
straight from the tube, achieve a sunny clarity
which suffuses the whole scene. The brushstrokes, varying from light to dense as the eye is
drawn across the dappled water, suggest movement and stillness in equal parts. The vertical
columns of the bridge, and the masts, secure the
two planes of the composition, so that despite its
insubstantial parts the painting conveys a feeling
of form as well as intense pleasure.

– an achievement he shares with Pissarro, who had also fled to London
(plate 30). Pissarro joined him in celebrating release from the tensions
at home not only by painting but also by seeking out the works of such
English masters as Turner and Constable. Later Pissarro was to recall
their enthusiasm for London as a painter's subject: 'Monet worked in
the parks, while I, living in Lower Norwood, studied the effect of fog,
snow and springtime . . . We also visited the museums. The watercolours and paintings of Constable and Turner and Old Crome certainly had an influence on us. We admired Gainsborough, Lawrence,
Reynolds etc., but we were struck chiefly by the landscape painters
who shared more our aim with regard to open-air, light and fugitive
effects.' Interesting though these observations are, Monet and Pissarro are unlikely to have seen the later Turner watercolours, and
certainly not the Constable oil sketches, which most powerfully evoke
the Impressionist idea to our modern eyes: they were nowhere to be
seen in public galleries at that time. It is, however, apparent that
these great English painters (and, less obviously, John Crome the
Norwich painter) encouraged them in their exile and reinforced their
convictions.

Another unexpected benefit from Monet's spell in London was an
introduction, through the French painter Daubigny, to the Paris dealer
Paul Durand-Ruel. He bought pictures from both Monet and Pissarro,
paying 200 and 300 francs each for them, five or six times as much as
they were used to getting in Paris, and then rarely enough.

Durand-Ruel deserves more than a passing mention. He was one of
those dealers, uncommon at any time, who elevate the dealer's role
above mere money-making. 'A genuine picture dealer,' he said, 'ought
to be at the same time an intelligent connoisseur, ready if need be to
sacrifice what seem to be his immediate interests to his artistic conviction. He should prefer to fight speculators rather than join in their
activities.' Between 1870 and 1875 he organised ten exhibitions in London including paintings by Manet, Monet, Sisley, Pissarro, Renoir and
Degas. He was attacked for exhibiting them, and some of his best clients
left him in disgust. He kept buying Impressionist paintings, though
they made no money for him. On returning to Paris after the 1870 war
he found the economic situation so bad that he was obliged to stop buying. To meet his bills he had to sell, at a loss, some fine works by Corot,
Delacroix, Millet, Rousseau, and other French masters. After gradually restoring his fortunes by careful dealing in the earlier painters he
began buying Impressionists again in 1880, then held a series of one-
man shows of Manet, Renoir, Pissarro and Sisley. By 1884 he was in
debt to the tune of a million francs. 'I would like to be free to go away
and live in a desert,' he confessed to Pissarro. Next year, 1885, he was
invited to organise the first Impressionist exhibition in New York. It
opened on 10th April, 1886: fifty works by Monet, forty-two by Pissarro, thirty-eight by Renoir, thirty-three by Degas, and others by
Manet, Boudin, Berthe Morisot, and Mary Cassatt. After a slow start

Plate 23 **The Thames below Westminster**

Plate 24 **The bridge at Argenteuil**

37

Plate 25
Claude Monet (1840–1926)
Springtime
1874
oil on canvas
$22\frac{1}{2} \times 31\frac{1}{2}$ in (57 × 80 cm)
Nationalgalerie, Berlin

Until they were dubbed 'Impressionists' Monet and his fellow painters regarded themselves as 'realists', the realism lying in their non-classical, non-literary interpretation of the everyday world. By 1874, the year of the first Impressionist exhibition and of this lyrical landscape by Monet, the movement was beginning to find its short-lived coherence. Monet, in particular, so mastered the techniques of shimmering luminosity that he was able to paint with unprecedented directness and speed.

and some hostile reviews, business began to pick up. Following a second New York exhibition in 1887, Durand-Ruel opened his own gallery there. By 1890 he was a rich man. By then, too, the tide had turned for most of the painters whom he had supported. 'You must not think Americans are savages,' he once wrote to Fantin-Latour. 'On the contrary, they are less ignorant and conservative than art-lovers in France . . .'

British reactions to the work of Monet and Pissarro were more cautious. Neither artist's work was accepted by the Royal Academy during their stay in London. Back in Paris, Monet and the other members of the group found life more difficult than ever. However they soon re-formed, and discussed an idea Bazille had originally suggested for by-passing the Salon and holding their own exhibition. This was the genesis of the Co-operative Society of Artists etc. already described, later to take its name from Monet's *Impression : sunrise*, painted in 1872.

Plate 26 **Impression: sunrise** *see plate 2*

And perhaps this is the point to consider the aims and attitudes which held such a disparate group together: the basic principles of Impressionism.

The word itself was not new when the critic of *Le Charivari*, Louis Leroy, threw it in the Society's face. Corot frequently used it to describe his own purposes in landscape. It occurs in Constable's writings, and in Turner's. Monet's friend Jongkind said that with him 'everything lies in the impression'. Its usefulness grew, however, as the cultural ripples from the artistic and social upheavals of the 1870s spread into other fields. Mallarmé came to be known as the Impressionist poet, and Debussy as an Impressionist composer. To the painters, it was a substitute for what are loosely regarded as the classic values which sustained art up till that time. It was essentially a rapid response to things seen, a glance, a quick glimpse from a half-closed eye, in which the painting, the impression, was the thing, not the sub-

Plate 27
Claude Monet (1840–1926)
The Gare St-Lazare
1877
oil on canvas
$32\frac{1}{4} \times 39\frac{3}{4}$ in (82 × 101 cm)
Fogg Art Museum, Harvard University,
Cambridge, Massachusetts (Bequest–Collection
of Maurice Wertheim)

Monet enjoyed telling the story of how, to dis-
prove his critics' contention that fog is not a subject for a painting, he set off one day in his best
suit for the Gare St-Lazare, where he introduced
himself to the station-master as 'Claude Monet,
the painter' and requested facilities to paint in
the station. The station-master, taking him for a
gentleman of the Salon, duly had the engines
recharged with coal to provide maximum smoke;
and when Monet had finished he was shown off
the premises with appropriate ceremony. The
experience provided Monet with the makings of a
masterpiece of Impressionism.

Plate 28
Claude Monet (1840–1926)
Waterlilies
1904
oil on canvas
$35\frac{1}{2} \times 36\frac{1}{4}$ in (90 × 92 cm)
Louvre, Paris

Monet's last great achievement was his series of
paintings of the waterlilies in his garden at
Giverny, where he spent the closing years of his
life. By then his struggle for recognition had been
won, and he could content himself in exploring
the frontiers between Impressionism and pure
abstraction. From the depths of the pool,
painted almost at eye-level–or, in his last years,
from directly overhead–he conjured lights,
shapes and colours as if from another world.
The pool, originally intended simply as an orna-
mental feature, became a secret universe in
which the aged painter, his strength and sight
failing, could find deep satisfaction and release.

ject itself. Hard outlines, precise detail, high finish–these were to be
avoided; they had no place in an image so fleetingly yet realistically
seen. The Impressionist eye was both descriptive and non-literal, a
conjunction which confused the spectator and irritated the critic.
There were no rules or standards to be offered as substitutes for conventional practices. Every painter had a right to make up his own rules,
if he needed any. The paint itself, the whole apparatus of making a
picture, played a dominant part in the whole. The trick was to give the
game away.

How it was done is epitomised, in Monet especially, by an extraordinary care for tone and colour. Light is everywhere, even in shadows; the Impressionist idea of shadow is simply a complementary
tone which includes the surrounding primary colours. Much use is
made of the white surface of the canvas, rather as in a watercolour, to
achieve an all-pervading sense of light. The brushwork tends to con-
sist of small dabs of colour, which work with one another to suggest
form. All this, so easy to recognise, demanded work both by the
painter and the viewer. Such brilliant simplifications forced a response
from the intelligence.

Certainly it was too much for the Salon, and Monet came to accept
the fact. The conflict between his painting and officially recognised
standards became impossible to reconcile. He and Renoir, who often
painted together in the 1860s, completed the process which had begun
a dozen years before, when Edouard Manet drew the crowds to the
Salon des Refusés.

For Monet the 1870s were a continual agony. A rich new patron,
Hoschedé, suddenly went bankrupt. Camille, who had lately had a

Plate 28 **Waterlilies**

second child, was in her last illness. When she died in 1879, Monet
set up house with his former patron's widow. It was the turning point
in his life. His new wife, a plump and practical thirty-nine-year-old,
had a nest-egg of her own. She also had a flair for dressmaking and
shrewd management. Monet's pictures began to sell. In 1889 he led
a movement to buy Manet's *Olympia* for the Louvre, and the following year he bought a solid property at Giverny. The rest of his life
brought continuing esteem as a painter, marred only by failing sight.
In his seventies he embarked on a series of paintings of waterlilies in
his garden at Giverny, some of which came close to pure abstract art
(plate 28). He was still painting at the age of eighty-six when he died.
Cézanne had said of him: 'Monet is only an eye. But what an eye!'
It has become his epitaph.

Plate 29 **Self-portrait**

Camille Pissarro

Every movement needs its theorist, a dedicated intelligence to give it continuity and direction. For the Impressionists this function was embodied in Camille Pissarro. He was older than any of them, and in speech and manner the most grave. His seniority gave him an authority which the younger men respected, even if, like them, he had to struggle to make ends meet. Though a convinced anarchist, who believed that the freedom of the artist is indivisible from the freedom of man, he was peaceable and sweet-tempered.

Pissarro was born in the Virgin Islands, the son of a Jewish-French shopkeeper of Spanish or Portuguese descent who sent him to be educated in Paris. There he decided to be a painter and after some exotic wanderings returned to Paris to enrol at the Ecole des Beaux Arts and the Académie Suisse. The Great Exhibition of 1855 opened his eyes to Corot, Daubigny and Courbet, who between them influenced his early landscapes. He was accepted at the Salon throughout the 1860s without, however, making much headway with the critics. One of them, commenting on his *Banks of the Marne in winter*, exhibited in 1866, called the treatment 'ugly and vulgar' and suggested that the artist was trying to be satirical. As Pissarro's style moved further from the Corot-esque, so his unsold pictures piled up; and as a father with other mouths to feed (he was living with a young woman who had been his mother's maid) he was forced to take odd jobs to earn money.

Like Monet, in 1870 he fled to England, where he had a half-sister. While he was there he heard that his little house in Louveciennes, outside Paris, had been used by the besieging Prussians as a butchery. Worse than that, his store of paintings had been put to use as duck-boards in the muddy garden. His meeting with Monet in London, and the encouragement of the good Daubigny, raised his spirits. The experience of exile seems to have hardened his ideas, not least since his enforced companionship with Monet brought him closer to the fold than he had been in Paris (plate 30). So far he had been trying to work out his own resolutions of style, palette and manner, while relating them to the example of living artists whose work he knew best, notably Corot, Daubigny and Courbet. Years before, Corot had told him: 'You are an artist. The only advice you need is this: study values. We don't see things the same way. You see green, I see grey and

Plate 29
Camille Pissarro (1831 – 1903)
Self-portrait
1873
oil on canvas
22 × 18¼ in (56 × 46 cm)
Louvre, Paris

43

Plate 30
Camille Pissarro (1831–1903)
Lower Norwood, London
1870
oil on canvas
13¾ × 18 in (34 × 45 cm)
National Gallery, London

Pissarro, the oldest of the original group, was also the most consistent in his loyalty to Impressionist ideas. Soon after arriving in Paris in 1855 he met Corot, whose style, and subsequently Courbet's, dominated his own work until 1870. In that year he struck up a close relationship with Monet, who was also in London to escape the war. On visits to the London collections both painters were encouraged by what they saw of the English landscape school, notably Turner and Constable, whose work in some ways anticipates Impressionism. Pissarro, delighted by the Victorian suburban landscape, began to paint in a direct Impressionist manner.

blond. But this is no reason for you not to work at values, because they above all are what one feels and experiences, and one can't make good paintings without them.' Now, with Monet at his elbow, Pissarro was better equipped to trust his own eye. He moved towards the simplicity and dignity which distinguish all but a handful of his most characteristic paintings, patiently adhering to the Impressionist attitudes to light, atmosphere, brushwork and paint.

Back in Paris the friends found things deeply depressing, despite the declaration of the new Republic. The same people seemed to be in positions of authority. There was censorship and favouritism, snobbery and reaction, just as before. Though the bourgeoisie seemed to have survived pretty well there was no money about, and little chance of finding patrons. The Salon was more reactionary than ever. Courbet had been fined and sent to prison for his part in the disturbances. Pissarro had lost most of his pictures. Bazille had not come back from the war.

Plate 31
Jean Baptiste Camille Corot (1796–1875)
L'entrée de village
about 1855
oil on canvas
$15\frac{3}{4} \times 12\frac{1}{4}$ in (40×31 cm)
Louvre, Paris

Impressionism probably owed as much to Corot as to any of the earlier French painters. Though he never gave the Impressionists his blessing as a group he exerted an important influence, especially on Pissarro, Renoir and Sisley. As the first French *plein-air* painter, he had a feeling for landscape based on both observation and emotion. As late as 1867, when he was seventy-one, he still felt a compulsion to go into the countryside and paint: 'In July, when I bury my nose in a hazel bush, I shall be fifteen years old again . . .' To the end of his life he remained capable of the strength and innocence which infuse this scene in the neighbourhood of Beauvais. He was revered into his old age, and beyond. At a mixed exhibition in 1897, by which time the Impressionist victory had been won, Monet declared: 'There is only one person here – Corot. The rest of us are nothing compared to him.'

Plate 32
Camille Pissarro (1831–1903)
The haystack, Pontoise
1873
oil on canvas
$18 \times 21\frac{1}{2}$ in (46×55 cm)
Durand-Ruel & Cie., Paris

On his return to France in June 1871, Pissarro moved from his war-ravaged home in Louveciennes to Pontoise. The honest naturalism of his painting, and its skilfully contained colour range, moved Cézanne to say in later years that if Pissarro had continued painting as he did in the 1870s 'he would have been the strongest of us all'.

Plate 33
Camille Pissarro (1831–1903)
Red roofs, edge of a village
1877
oil on canvas
$21 \times 25\frac{1}{4}$ in (53×64 cm)
Louvre, Paris

This painting of a village skirted by a wood, seen in a winter light, ranks as one of the masterpieces of Pissarro's best period. The adventurous directness with which he has approached a complicated subject, and the subtle balancing of bright tones, succeed in conveying a sense of a real place rather than being merely a dazzling exercise in colour and design.

Plate 34
Camille Pissarro (1831–1903)
Grey day on the banks of the Oise
1878
oil on canvas
$21\frac{1}{4} \times 25\frac{1}{2}$ in (54 × 65 cm)
Louvre, Paris

Many of Pissarro's most distinguished paintings are in relatively subdued tones which, far from lacking the force of strong colour, accentuate the brighter shades in naturalistic landscapes. The grey day has not produced a grey picture. Pissarro may have lacked Monet's 'fantastic eye', as the critic Theodore Doret called it, but his deep-seated feeling for nature enabled him to state truths in his landscapes which arose from his own sensibility.

Pissarro now began spending time with Cézanne, whom he had first met ten years before, and helped to lure him away from the thickly masculine, Romantic style of Courbet to the lighter Impressionist manner. Cézanne learned from Pissarro, while painting alongside him on walks in the country north of Paris, the secrets of broken brushstrokes and enveloping light. For the third Impressionist exhibition, in April 1877, Pissarro and his colleagues on the hanging committee gave Cézanne the best positions. Only Pissarro between 1874 and 1886 exhibited at every one of the eight Impressionist exhibitions, sticking to the task when his friends wavered or grew bored. Durand-Ruel did his best to stir up interest. 'He runs around doing all he can to push us,' Pissarro wrote to Monet in 1883. 'It's quite understandable that other dealers and speculators should say he can only last a week . . .'

Pissarro's example, and his selfless support of younger painters, including Gauguin and Van Gogh, won for him a special place in the Impressionists' affections. His intellectual curiosity attracted him for a time to the pointillist techniques of Seurat and his disciples (plate 65), but he returned to Impressionism with his powers enhanced and proceeded to paint some of his finest work. He had to wait until nearly the end of his life for recognition. In 1892 a retrospective exhibition of his work, organised by Durand-Ruel, established him among the great painters of the age. Gauguin, ten years later, paid tribute to his 'extreme artistic will' and his 'essentially intuitive, well-bred air,' adding, 'He was one of my masters, and I do not deny him.' Cézanne, a man of sparing eloquence, said: 'Perhaps we all come from Pissarro.' He died in Paris on 12th November 1903, having produced a vast quantity of work in a variety of techniques.

Plate 35
Camille Pissarro (1831–1903)
The Boulevard Montmartre
1897, oil on canvas, $13\frac{3}{4} \times 17\frac{3}{4}$ in (35 × 45 cm)
Mr and Mrs John Loeb Collection, New York

Pissarro was the only Impressionist to support every one of the group's exhibitions from 1874 onwards. The last one was in 1886, by which time most of the group had begun to go their separate ways. Pissarro then became attracted to the quasi-scientific theory of divisionism (or pointillism) propounded – and successfully demonstrated – by George Seurat. But Pissarro returned to the methods he knew and trusted, painting in his last years some of the most satisfying work of his life. His *Boulevard Montmartre* is an evocative and endearing study of Paris in the spring.

Plate 36 **Portrait of Berthe Morisot**

Berthe Morisot

A popular and attractive member of the painters' circle during their formative years was Berthe Morisot. Her intelligence, sensibility and high qualities as a painter endeared her to the young Impressionists, who treated her as an equal: 'that great lady' as Renoir called her. Perhaps Renoir was mindful of the fact that Berthe Morisot was a great-granddaughter of Fragonard, one of his favourite French painters; but her talents and beauty would in any case have earned her an honoured place in the Impressionist fraternity. Her natural abilities were refined by a succession of good teachers, including Corot. Through him she was introduced to some of the leading painters of the time, and her family's social position ensured that she met a variety of notable personages likely to be useful in furthering her career as a painter. Her first submission to the Salon in 1864, when she was twenty-three, was accepted, and she exhibited there without a break for the next nine years. In the meantime she had met the members of Manet's circle, and felt strongly drawn to them, especially to Manet himself. She took a leading part in organising the first Impressionist exhibition in 1874, in which she showed nine works, though Manet was hotly opposed both to it and to Berthe's involvement.

Along with the others, she was to feel the lash of the critics' scorn. After the second Impressionist exhibition in 1876 the critic of *Le Figaro*, Albert Wolff, penned his oft-quoted notice. 'The innocent pedestrian,' he wrote, 'attracted by the flags outside, goes in for a look. But what a cruel spectacle meets his frightened eyes! Five or six lunatics—one of them a woman—make up a group of poor wretches who have succumbed to the madness of ambition and dared to put on an exhibition of their work . . . There is a woman in the group, as in all well-known gangs. Her name is Berthe Morisot, and she is a curiosity. She manages to convey a certain feminine grace despite her outbursts of delirium.' The men were furious at these insults to Berthe Morisot, but, Renoir recalled later, 'she just laughed'.

Her close relationship with Manet dated from 1868, when she was copying a Rubens in the Louvre and Fantin-Latour introduced her. Manet asked her to pose for him in a picture he had in mind, *The balcony*, which duly appeared in the Salon the following year. She quickly became an intimate part of his life, though evidently not his mistress: Manet was contentedly married to his plump and comfort-

Plate 36
Edouard Manet (1832–83)
Portrait of Berthe Morisot
1872
oil on canvas
$21\frac{3}{4} \times 15$ in (53×38 cm)
Rouart Collection, Paris

Manet's gift for portraiture produced memorable studies of people prominent in his life and affections, such as Duret, Zola, Mallarmé and other members of his circle. His relations with Berthe Morisot, herself a gifted artist and a regular exhibitor at the Salon until 1873, drew him closer to the Impressionists, whose cause she took up with enthusiasm and courage. They, in their turn, treated her with chivalrous affection all her life. Berthe Morisot, after becoming Manet's pupil, married his brother Eugène. Manet painted her several times, always with a tender appreciation of her womanliness and beauty.

Plate 37
Berthe Morisot (1841–95)
The harbour at Lorient
1869
oil on canvas
17 × 28¾ in (43 × 73 cm)
National Gallery of Art,
Washington (Ailsa Mellon
Bruce Collection)

Early in her career Berthe Morisot worked with Corot, who was a regular visitor at her parents' home in Passy. But it was Manet who became the major influence in her life. She had known him for a year when she painted this picture, posing her sister Edma on the harbour wall at Lorient. At the same time she was not too happy at the attentions Manet was paying to his new pupil: 'Manet lectures me, and holds up that eternal Mlle Gonzalès as an example . . . whereas I am not capable of anything.' However, Manet so admired this painting that Berthe Morisot at once made him a present of it.

Plate 38
Berthe Morisot (1841–95)
In the dining room
1886
oil on canvas
24¼ × 19¾ in (61 × 50 cm)
National Gallery of Art, Washington

In the year in which this picture was painted the
Impressionists held their last group exhibition.
Berthe Morisot had fourteen paintings in that
exhibition, which she helped to organise. In that
year, too, Durand-Ruel held the first Impressionist exhibition in New York, in which Berthe
Morisot was also represented. That she more
than held her own in the other Impressionists'
company may be seen from the vigorous orig-
inality of this painting, in which the apparent
disorder of the setting in no way detracts from
the feminine charm of the young housewife. This
was a seventeen-year-old model, Isabelle Lam-
bert, of whom Berthe Morisot was particularly
fond, and who was to die tragically young.

Plate 39
Berthe Morisot (1841–95)
Woman at her toilet
about 1875
oil on canvas
23¾ × 31¼ in (60 × 80 cm)
Art Institute of Chicago (Stickney Fund)

This is one of fifteen paintings which Berthe
Morisot showed at the fifth Impressionist exhibition, held in the Rue des Pyramides, Paris,
in 1880. Her painterly sensibility, which never
deserted her, enabled her to paint decorative
subjects without lapsing into mere picture-
making. Her home became a favourite meeting
place of her fellow painters, and of many of the
younger literary figures of the time.

able Suzanne. Nevertheless, it seems likely that Berthe would willing-
ly have spent her life with him. A sense of propriety on his part, and
good manners on hers, held them apart. This situation lasted for six
years, in which Berthe felt her youth beginning to slip away. She de-
sired marriage, and came upon a happy solution: she married Manet's
younger brother, Eugène. She wrote to her brother: 'I have found an
honest and excellent man who I think loves me sincerely. I am facing
the realities of life . . .' Their home in the Rue de Villejust became a
favourite rendezvous of the Impressionists and their friends, for Berthe
Morisot attracted good minds and good company.

Berthe Morisot's own work shows the influence of Manet, though

Plate 39 **Woman at her toilet**

it is generally softer and looser in execution and lighter in palette. The dominant characteristic is perhaps its womanliness, the aspect of her own nature which, more even than her intelligence and talent, made the Impressionists love her. Before she died in 1895 she asked Renoir to take care of her daughter Julie and her nieces Jeanie and Paule. Julie in due course married the painter Georges Rouault, and Jeanie the poet Paul Valéry. Jean Renoir, the painter's son, who knew them all, wrote: 'Whenever I have an opportunity to go and see [these] old friends, I feel as if I were breathing a more subtle air than elsewhere, a remnant of the breeze which stirred gently through the Manet drawing room: a breath of the Parnassian wind . . .'

Plate 40 **Portrait of Renoir**

Pierre Auguste Renoir

Renoir's position among the Impressionists, like that of Manet and Degas, is somewhat contradictory. On the one hand he produced, over a period of some ten years, works which are the quintessence of Impressionism. On the other hand, he was deeply aware of the long pedigree of European painting, and wanted to be part of it. He revered such masters as Veronese, Titian and (like Manet) Velazquez, and delighted in such eighteenth-century French predecessors as Watteau, Boucher and Fragonard. 'Those bourgeois women of Fragonard's! They are distinguished and at the same time good-natured. You hear them speak the French of our fathers . . .' When he finished his late masterpiece, *Les grandes baigneuses*, he declared: 'Rubens would have been satisfied with it.' For Renoir, there could be no higher satisfaction.

He was born at Limoges, the son of a tailor, who brought the family to Paris when Renoir was four. There was no parental resistance to the idea that their son might be a painter. As a first step, he took a job painting flowers on pieces of chinaware for five sous a dozen. On evening visits to the Louvre he discovered the masters. Just as he was looking forward to graduating to the rank of porcelain painter at six francs a day, a mechanical process was discovered which put his employer out of business. So he took to painting fans, decorating them with copies he made in the Louvre of subjects by Watteau, Lancret and Boucher.

It was not long before he took the logical step of attending art classes. He enrolled with Charles Gleyre, whose pupils included Monet, Bazille and Sisley, and at the Ecole des Beaux Arts for life drawing and anatomy. His first important paintings were figure subjects and portraits, including a vivid study of Bazille, perhaps the closest friend of his early days. With Monet he often painted on the banks of the Seine. The two men's versions of La Grenouillère in 1869 are strikingly alike with their flickering brushwork, informal composition and sunny colour. Renoir's interest in the human figure seems to have influenced Monet's versions, which in turn made an evident mark on his companion's poetic imagination. Renoir was always impatient of theory, and tended to drop out of earnest conversations which threatened to keep him up late. Composition, he felt, should be as varied as nature. 'The eyes of the most beautiful faces,'

Plate 40
Frédéric Bazille (1841–71)
Portrait of Renoir
1867
oil on canvas
24¾ × 20 in (62 × 51 cm)
Musée des Beaux Arts, Algiers

The example of Manet is again to be seen in this portrait, in which Bazille returns the compliment by depicting Renoir in what was surely a characteristic attitude, restlessly poised between thought and action. It ranks as one of Bazille's most successful compositions.

Plate 41 **Le Moulin de la Galette**

he observed, 'are always slightly dissimilar. No nose is found exactly above the middle of the mouth. The segments of an orange, the leaves of a tree, or the petals of a flower are never identical.'

Renoir exhibited with his friends at the Impressionist exhibitions of 1874 and 1876, and suffered the general critical mauling. Though he was as hard-up as Monet, he chose to earn what he could by doing hack work at his old trade. Always the most cheerful and resilient of the group, he revelled in the life of the cafés and boulevards, the river picnics and the company of friends, all of which he celebrated in paint. In 1874, with Manet and Monet, he brought Impressionism to perhaps its highest pitch of inventive artistry. Monet had a home-made floating studio on the river at Argenteuil. There, Manet painted him at work (plate 1) while Renoir recorded almost identical scenes. Their pictures have more in common than the spirit in which they were painted; the colours are made up of their constituent parts, laid side by side on the canvas, and there are no outlines or hard shadows. Land and water coalesce in a way not seen in painting before, yet with brilliant conviction: in Monet's phrase, ensnaring the light and throwing it directly on to the canvas.

Paintings of this character did not find buyers. Renoir's son Jean, in his biography of his father, tells how all the money the two friends could scrape together went to pay for their studio, a model and coal for the stove. The stove served two purposes: to warm the girls while cooking the food. One of their sitters chanced to be a grocer, who paid them in kind. They could make a sack of beans last a month. Renoir said of those days: 'I have never been happier in my life.' Of his work in those Impressionist years, the *Moulin de la Galette*, exhibited in the 1877 exhibition, is his acknowledged masterpiece (plate 41). In it, as Renoir's friend Georges Rivière justly observed, there is 'noise, laughter, movement, sun and an atmosphere of youth'. His review went on: 'It is essentially a Parisian work. The girls are the very same who elbow us every day and whose babble fills Paris at certain hours. A smile and a flick of the wrist is enough to be pretty; M. Renoir proves it.' Prophetically, in a reference to the kind of historical subjects which still dominated the Salon, he added: 'When, for the hundredth time, we are shown St Louis dealing out justice under an oak, are we the better for it? What documents will these artists who deliver us from such lucubrations bequeath to future centuries...'

The sheer sense of pleasure inherent in Renoir's work might well have been a factor in helping to turn the critical tide. The Impressionists had no clique to speak up for them. Their friend and champion Emile Zola was for years a lone voice. The praise of other writers came only after they had achieved recognition and no longer needed it.

Renoir did, however, have one devoted critic in his brother Edmond, an aspiring writer who became managing editor of a newspaper, *La Vie Moderne*, started by the distinguished publisher Charpentier. Renoir had painted Charpentier's mother in 1869, and the family were well disposed towards him and his friends. Charpentier, having bought Renoir's *Fisherman on a river bank* for 180 francs, invited the painter to his house, where such writers as Zola, Maupassant and the Goncourt brothers were welcome guests. Renoir was charmed by the household, and delightedly painted the young daughters who, he said, reminded him of Fragonard. 'I was able to forget the journalists' abuse. I had not only free models but obliging ones.' Edmond, with access to Charpentier's newspaper, wrote several articles in support of the Impressionist painters, his brother in particular. One of these, written in 1879, gives an account of Renoir's methods as a painter. To Renoir, wrote Edmond, the forests of Fontainebleau were better than the four walls of a studio. 'Atmosphere and surroundings had an enormous influence on him. Having no memory of the kind of servitude to which artists so often bind themselves, he let himself be set in

Plate 41
Pierre Auguste Renoir (1841–1919)
Le Moulin de la Galette
1876
oil on canvas
30¾ × 45 in (78 × 114 cm)
Louvre, Paris

One of Renoir's undoubted masterpieces, this painting was glowingly reviewed by Georges Rivière in the first number of *L'Impressionniste* in April 1877. Renoir and his group, he noted, had discovered that narrative painting 'is not just the illustration of droll stories from the past: they have opened up a way which others will certainly follow'. Renoir painted this large picture on the spot, over a number of days, posing his friends in the pleasure gardens and co-opting any girls who might chance to join them. The result is a triumphantly happy painting and a resounding declaration of what Impressionism stood for at this date.

Plate 42
Pierre Auguste Renoir (1841–1919)
At La Grenouillère
1869
oil and canvas
26 × 31¾ in (66 × 80 cm)
Nationalmuseum, Stockholm

Renoir's versions of the subjects which he and Monet painted side by side (plate 21) confirm the bond which existed between them when the first principles of Impressionism were being discovered, with mounting excitement, in suburban surroundings and ordinary events. Renoir was at this time penniless, but undismayed. The experience of La Grenouillère had given him a new vision.

Plate 43 **Nude in sunlight**

motion by his subjects, and above all by the character of the place he was in.' He continued:

'That is the particular quality of his work: he re-stated it everywhere and at all times, from *Lise*, painted in the forest, to the portrait of *Mme Charpentier and her children*, which was painted in her home without the furniture being moved from its normal daily position, and without anything being prepared to give more importance to one part of the picture than another. When he painted the *Moulin de la Galette* he settled down to it for six months, wedded to this whole world which so enchanted him, and for which models in poses were not good enough. Immersing himself in this whirlpool of pleasure-seeking, he captured the hectic moment with dazzling vivacity. When he painted a portrait he asked his sitter to keep his ordinary clothes, to sit as he always did in his usual position, so that nothing should look uncomfortable or prepared . . .

'In following my brother's whole output one realises there is no "method". In none of his works does one find the same way of procedure, yet they hold together all the way through by aiming not as perfection of surface but at complete understanding of natural harmony.'

Renoir's total refusal to be bound by systems and methods, particularly those urged on him by others, is an essential element in his work. When the painter Laporte told him, 'You must force yourself to draw,' Renoir replied: 'I am like a little cork thrown in the water and carried by the current. I let myself paint as it comes to me.' Gleyre, his teacher, examining a sketch Renoir was working on, said: 'Young man, you are very skilful, very gifted. But no doubt you took up painting just to amuse yourself.' Renoir replied: 'Certainly. If it didn't amuse me I wouldn't be doing it.' Degas, who had a lifelong respect for form, regarded Renoir as a law unto himself: 'He can do anything he likes.'

Renoir did not exhibit with the Impressionists in 1879 and 1881. Instead he began to travel, first to Algeria for six months, then to Guernsey, and in 1881 to Italy with his young bride Aline Charigot. The experience of Italy impressed and unsettled him. Was Impressionism, after all, a satisfactory end in itself? A painter friend of his with similar doubts, Paul Cézanne, seemed to think not. In 1883 Renoir decided that his art must take another direction. 'I had come to the end of Impressionism, and had arrived at a situation in which I did not know how to paint or draw,' he confessed later. After a period of introspection and experiment he visited Spain in 1886, though briefly, because, as he said, 'When you have seen Velazquez you lose all desire to paint. You realise everything has already been said.'

From now on his style broadened into the loose, flowing, sensuous manner for which he is probably best known: the period of the great nudes and of his glorification of life and Nature. By then the other

Plate 43
Pierre Auguste Renoir (1841–1919)
Nude in sunlight
about 1875
oil on canvas
$31\frac{1}{2} \times 25\frac{1}{2}$ in (80 × 61 cm)
Louvre, Paris

There is no mistaking the difference between natural light, in which this study was painted, and the flat light of a painter's studio. In his celebrations of womanly beauty Renoir liked to suggest the ripeness of young flesh warmed by the sun, the skin surfaces reflecting a light which is itself aglow with life. Vincent van Gogh wrote to his brother Theo from Provence: 'I think very often of Renoir and that pure, clean line of his. That's just how things and people look in this clear air.'

Plate 44
Pierre Auguste Renoir (1841–1919)
The umbrellas
about 1884
oil on canvas
$71 \times 45\frac{1}{4}$ in (180 × 114 cm)
National Gallery, London

Renoir gradually abandoned, or modified, the more purist aspects of Impressionism, moving towards deliberate form and geometric composition. This distinguished painting shows his skill in the disposition of shapes, still seemingly natural but carefully worked out to achieve rhythm and poise, holding the apparently random conjunction of faces, movements and gestures in almost classical balance. There is still a strong Impressionist element, however, in the total absence of black from the shadows.

Plate 45
Pierre Auguste Renoir (1841–1919)
Two girls reading in a garden
about 1890
oil on canvas
$18\frac{3}{4} \times 21\frac{3}{4}$ in (46 × 55 cm)
Private collection, Paris

Renoir made several versions of this study, including pastels and etchings, *Le chapeau épinglé*, for which the model was Berthe Morisot's daughter. The painting is in Renoir's opulent, late Impressionist manner, in which full value is given to the most striking colours and the lines flow into one another without interruption. The intimacy of the pose, the absorption of the two young faces, and the melting harmonies of Renoir's palette all combine to produce an endearing study of girlish innocence.

Plate 44 **The umbrellas** *see page 63*

Plate 45 **Two girls reading in a garden** *see page 63*

Impressionists had broken up, the impulse which had held them together having all but died out. Renoir entered into an honoured and productive old age, working to the last with brushes taped to his arthritic wrists. 'With such hands, how do you paint?' a journalist asked him towards the end of his life. 'With my prick,' answered the old man. Nobody laughed. He died at Cagnes on 17th December, 1919.

Plate 46 **Portrait of Frédéric Bazille**

Frédéric Bazille

Jean Frédéric Bazille, who met Monet and Renoir at Gleyre's and became a popular member of their circle, came of an upper class family in Montpellier. His parents envisaged a conventional career for him, and for a time he obliged them by studying medicine in Paris as well as art. As a well-to-do young man up from the provinces he was fascinated by Paris and its teeming, disorderly life. He shared his studio with Monet, who must have been a difficult companion to live with even for someone as politely long-suffering as Bazille. Monet's poverty was partly relieved by Bazille's generously buying a painting from him, *Women in a garden*, for 2,500 francs, which he paid at the rate of 50 francs a month. When Monet brought Camille, his pregnant mistress, to live with him, Bazille soon found himself looking after her too. The equally penniless Renoir also spent the winter of 1866 under Bazille's roof. Their gently bred friend was also useful to Monet and Renoir through his social contacts and his access to family cash when things were at their worst.

Monet constantly urged Bazille to get out of Paris and paint in the open air. He wrote to him from Honfleur in July 1864: 'I keep asking myself what you could possibly be doing in Paris in such beautiful weather. Here, my friend, it is beautiful and every day I discover more beautiful things. I am going mad because I want to do everything . . . I want to stuggle, destroy and begin again, because one can do what one wants and understands. When I look at nature it seems to me that I see it all made, completely written out. Afterwards, when it comes to getting it down yourself and you're actually working on it, that's when the going gets rough!' He did manage to lure Bazille into the woods of Fontainebleau to pose for his *Déjeuner sur l'herbe*, a tribute to Manet's version of the subject, with Camille.

Bazille's own work never developed into Impressionism; he was too preoccupied with traditional form and structure, and his paintings were based on careful drawings and studies. Renoir's portrait of Bazille, painted in 1867, is one of his most successful works of this period, showing how thoroughly he had mastered the example of Manet—who, appropriately enough, bought the picture for himself (plate 46). Bazille's portrait of Renoir in the same year shows his talent at its best; the pose, and the curiously vibrant character of the young Renoir, combine to make this perhaps the most successful

Plate 46
Pierre Auguste Renoir (1841–1919)
Portrait of Frédéric Bazille
1867
oil on canvas
$41\frac{3}{4} \times 29$ in (106 × 74 cm)
Louvre, Paris

Renoir's affectionate study of the companion of his early days captures the gravity and slight awkwardness of the exceptionally tall young painter at work. The style is more reminiscent of Courbet than of Renoir's own circle at this time, though there is a strong suggestion of Manet's influence in the construction. Manet, in fact, bought the painting from Renoir: as much, one likes to think, out of regard for the sitter as in recognition of its qualities. Three years later, before he could build on his early promise, Bazille was dead, killed in the French retreat from the Prussians at Beaune-la-Rolande, aged twenty-nine.

Plate 47
Frédéric Bazille (1841–71)
Family reunion
1869
oil on canvas
60 × 91½ in (152 × 232 cm)
Louvre, Paris

This ambitious exercise in group portraiture derives largely from Monet, whom Bazille greatly admired and with whom he shared his studio. Bazille owned Monet's painting on a similar theme, *Women in a garden*, painted in 1866, which he paid for by instalments to help his friend's finances.

Plate 48
Frédéric Bazille (1841–71)
La toilette
1870
oil on canvas
52 × 50 in (132 × 127 cm)
Musée Fabre, Montpellier

Bazille, though closely associated with the young Impressionists in work and friendship, remained more true to the classical tradition in design. This painting owes as much to Delacroix, whom Bazille greatly admired, as to Manet's *Olympia* or Renoir's *Odalisque*, a costume painting in the Delacroix manner. Other figure paintings of Bazille's do, however, indicate that he might have gone on to greater things had his life not been cut short in the year this picture was painted.

picture Bazille ever painted (plate 40). There is also much interest in *The artist's studio, Rue de la Condamine*, painted in 1870. It shows a spacious studio with figures, one of which—the tall Bazille—was painted in afterwards by Monet, who is shown looking at a canvas on the easel with Monet standing by. In the same year the Salon accepted Bazille's *Summer scene* (Bathers), now in the Fogg Art Museum, Harvard.

When the war of 1870 broke out, nearly all the young painters scattered to avoid being caught up in it. Bazille was one of those who stayed in Paris. He enrolled in the Zouaves, a dashing regiment of light infantry. On 28th November, 1870, he was killed at Beaune-la-Rolande. He was twenty-nine. Renoir remembered him: 'That gentle knight, so pure in heart; the friend of my youth.'

Plate 49 **Alfred Sisley and his wife**

Alfred Sisley

Alfred Sisley has the distinction of being grouped with Monet and Pissarro as one of the most consistently 'pure' Impressionists. Compared with their work, his may sometimes seem to lack the hard centre which is one of the marks of a master; but he set himself the same standards, and many of his paintings rank among the most successful work produced even by the band of geniuses who befriended him. He was an Englishman, born in Paris in 1839 and brought up there until he was eighteen, when his family sent him to London to equip himself for a career in business. After four years he persuaded them to let him return to Paris and be a painter. For a few months he was one of the group at Gleyre's which included Monet, Renoir and Bazille, but he soon began to spend most of his time painting in the countryside at Fontainebleau, Marlotte and St Cloud. He did not, however, cut himself off from the young painters he had met at Gleyre's; he went on several painting excursions with Monet, and also worked with both Renoir and Bazille.

During these early years he was under the influence of Corot, and his work shows little of the inventiveness which was already beginning to separate Monet and Renoir, in particular, from the rest of the group. He had two works accepted at the Salon in 1866, but it was not until the 1870s that he achieved the balance between tone and form which distinguishes his best-known work. The Corot influence never quite left him, but once he turned to painting in earnest (his father's business having failed after the 1870 war, obliging Sisley to paint for his living) his work assumed a noticeably more professional quality.

With the characteristically light Impressionist palette and quick, short brushstrokes, Sisley became a brilliant exponent of atmospheric effects (plate 51). Shy and diffident by nature, he retreated into suburban domesticity, always short of money, striving for the recognition which would relieve his family of the spartan poverty in which they lived. Over a period of twenty years he produced many paintings which for sensitivity and lyricism challenge comparison with Monet or Pissarro. His snow scenes, and his studies of mists and floods, show a marvellous subtlety and understanding of tones. He was one of the small group including Monet, Renoir and Berthe Morisot who tried their luck by putting some of their paintings up for auction at the

Plate 49
Pierre Auguste Renoir (1841–1919)
Alfred Sisley and his wife
1868
oil on canvas
$29\frac{1}{2} \times 41\frac{1}{4}$ in (75 × 105 cm)
Wallraf-Richartz Museum, Cologne

The Impressionists, when painting one another's portraits, usually managed to convey the affectionate comradeship which held them together. Renoir's portrait of Sisley and his newly wedded bride pays them both a charming compliment: Sisley in his handsome and stylish suit, his pretty young wife in a splendidly striped gown of orange and yellow, leaning tenderly on his arm.

Plate 50
Alfred Sisley (1839–99)
The small meadows in spring
about 1885
oil on canvas
$21\frac{1}{4} \times 28\frac{3}{4}$ in (54×73 cm)
Tate Gallery, London

In the 1880s Sisley began to make use of brighter colours, though not always so successfully as in this appealing study of a fresh spring landscape along the river near his home at Moret-sur-Loing. By now he was a thoroughly professional artist, having been forced by the failure of his father's business following the war of 1870 to turn to painting as a livelihood. During much of his later life his only support came from fellow painters and from the dealer Durand-Ruel, who bought pictures from him with no expectation that they would sell. In the last days of his life Sisley appealed to Monet to look after his children. The subsequent sale of the paintings from his studio was a success. Within a year of his death, Sisley took his rightful place beside Monet, Renoir and Pissarro.

Drouot Galleries in 1874, an occasion which ended in one outraged spectator calling Berthe Morisot a streetwalker. Pissarro punched him in the face, a brawl started, and someone called the police. Not a single picture was sold

Durand-Ruel supported Sisley by buying his paintings, though there was no demand for them even at a time when the other Impressionists were beginning to find eager buyers. In January 1899 Sisley, sick and worn out, asked Monet to come and see him, requesting him

Plate 51
Alfred Sisley (1839–99)
Misty morning
1874
oil on canvas
20 × 25½ in (50 × 65 cm)
Louvre, Paris

A landscape of this insubstantial quality would have been virtually impossible before Impressionism. Nothing is explicit, yet everything is clear: the all-enveloping haze, the figure of the woman seemingly afloat in a spray of mist, the outlines of the fruit trees, the blooms in the foreground catching the first pale rays of the sun.

Plate 52
Alfred Sisley (1839–99)
Barge during the flood
1876
oil on canvas
19¾ × 24 in (50 × 61 cm)
Louvre, Paris

Sisley painted three versions of this subject, one of which was shown at the second Impressionist exhibition in 1876. Sisley's work may often lack the electric energy of Monet or Renoir, but it is suffused with a calm lyricism which was a mark of his own temperament. He was particularly sensitive to low-toned landscape subjects, and paid attention to his skies. 'The sky cannot be merely a background,' he wrote, 'it contributes movement by its form.' Sisley remained true to Impressionism all his life, sometimes treating parts of his pictures in varying styles, as in the firm lines of the buildings in this otherwise purely atmospheric composition.

to look after his wife and children. A week later he died. Monet helped to organise a sale of the paintings left in Sisley's studio, as a means of raising money for his destitute family. Dealers and collectors descended on the Sisleys' little home at Moret-sur-Loing, near Fontainebleau. Everything was sold. Within a year, a painting for which Sisley had once accepted 100 francs was sold for 45,000. It was *The flood at Port Marly*, one of three versions which Sisley painted of that subject in 1876 (plate 52). It is now in the Louvre.

Plate 51 **Misty morning** *see page* 73

Plate 52 **Barge during the flood** *see page* 73

Mary Cassatt

From the time of the fourth Impressionist exhibition in 1879 the youngest member of the group was an American painter, Mary Cassatt. Paris exerted a strong attraction for well-bred young ladies with a taste for life in the artists' quarter (in Jean Renoir's biography of his father there is the story of an English girl student who pressed Gleyre to have the male model take his little pants off), but Mary Cassatt is not to be numbered among the typical mid-nineteenth-century art students portrayed in Murger's *Scènes de la Bohème* or Du Maurier's *Trilby*. She had served four years at the Pennsylvania Academy of Fine Arts before setting off for Europe in 1866 at the age

Plate 53
Edgar Degas (1834–1917)
At the milliner's
about 1882
pastel
$27\frac{1}{2} \times 27\frac{3}{4}$ in (69 × 70 cm)
Museum of Modern Art, New York (Gift of Mrs David M. Levy)

The interest in photographic composition which distinguishes much of Degas' work is clearly evident in this naturalistic study, for which Mary Cassatt posed as the customer trying on hats. Mary Cassatt's long friendship with Degas is commemorated in numerous paintings by him in which she appears.

Plate 54 **The little sisters**

of twenty-one. Far from embracing the life-style of American students in Paris, she found it objectionable. She seems to have found her own way to Manet's work, though there is nothing particularly adventurous about the paintings she submitted to the Salon in 1872 and the following two years. She then met Degas, becoming his model and, more importantly, his friend. Degas, never an easy man to deal with, became very attached to her. Perhaps they were lovers; certainly they worked closely together, discovered Japanese prints, and shared a taste for classic draughtsmanship. She exhibited with the Impressionists in 1879, their fourth appearance as a group, and in all subsequent years except 1882, when she withdrew in sympathy with

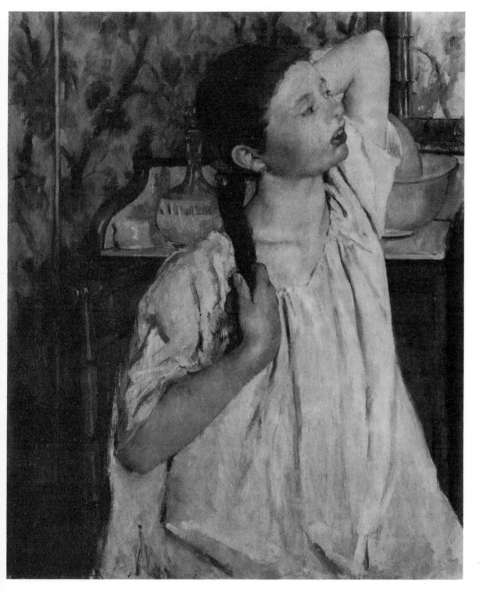

Plate 54
Mary Cassatt (1844–1926)
The little sisters
about 1885
oil on canvas
$18 \times 21\frac{1}{2}$ in (45×55 cm)
Glasgow Art Gallery

Mary Cassatt, born of a wealthy Pittsburgh family, settled in Paris in 1868 to study painting. In 1877 she met Degas, through whom she entered the world of the Impressionists, exhibiting with them four times between 1879 and 1886. Degas influenced her style as a painter, but her happiest works have an unforced naturalism which is entirely her own.

Plate 55
Mary Cassatt (1844–1926)
Girl arranging her hair
1886
oil on canvas
$29\frac{1}{2} \times 24\frac{1}{2}$ in (75×62 cm)
National Gallery of Art, Washington
(Chester Dale Collection)

At one time owned by Degas, this painting was included in the Impressionists' eighth exhibition, held in 1886, for which rooms were hired above a well-known Paris restaurant, the Maison Dorée. Monet, Renoir and Sisley chose not to exhibit, and after some argument Seurat, Signac and Pissarro were assigned a room to themselves. In the same year the dealer Durand-Ruel held the first Impressionist exhibition in New York, encouraged by Mary Cassatt, whose efforts to interest her fellow Americans in Impressionist painting did much to further their subsequent success.

Degas who was at that time feuding with the committee. Renoir, who did not care much for women painters (though he made an exception of Berthe Morisot) got on well with her. He once met her in Brittany on a painting expedition, noting that 'she carried her easel like a man'.

Her work has considerable feminine charm and fluency without resorting to unduly sentimental subjects. She was both wealthy enough to buy the Impressionists' work when their prices began to rise, and candid enough to criticise it. She once told Renoir that his technique was 'too simple', adding: 'The public don't like that.' Renoir's reply was typical. 'Don't worry,' he told her, 'complicated theories can always be thought up *afterwards*.'

Plate 56 **Self-portrait**

Paul Cézanne

Two paintings in the first Impressionist exhibition of 1874 announced the presence of a new force: Paul Cézanne. The first showed a woman half crouching, half sprawling on a bed, her nudity abruptly exposed by an apparently naked negress plucking back the coverlet while a clothed and bearded onlooker gazed up at her from a deep divan. It was called *A modern Olympia*, an obvious derivation from Manet's notorious exhibit in the Salon of 1865 (plates 6,57). The other was a painting executed largely with the palette knife, of a house and farm buildings bathed in soft golden sunlight, called *The House of the Hanged Man* (plate 58). Each, in its own degree, forced itself on the spectator: the *Olympia* with its eroticism, its distortions, and its violent, slapdash colours; and the landscape with its fierce honesty of tone and composition. The critic of the journal *L'Artiste*, while letting Monet, Renoir and Degas off lightly, called the *Olympia* 'a nightmare' and Cézanne a 'bit of a madman, afflicted with painting delirium tremens,' adding: 'No audacity can surprise us. But when it comes to landscapes M. Cézanne will allow us to pass in silence over his *House of the Hanged Man . . .*'

Cézanne can hardly have been surprised, or unduly disappointed. For years he had been trying to get accepted at the Salon, though his chances were not improved by his habit of trundling his work round in a barrow, dressed like a hawker, to demonstrate his contempt for the whole proceedings. The *Modern Olympia*, even to a twentieth-century eye, seems almost wilfully provocative: a sardonic jest, a *jeu d'ésprit* with a sting in it. The *House of the Hanged Man*, though considerably less outrageous in subject, lumped Cézanne with Pissarro and Monet. (It found a buyer, however: Victor Chocquet, a lowly customs official who had already begun to buy Impressionists.) Taken together, the two works conveniently sum up the kind of painter Cézanne already was, and the fervent, contradictory nature which was to lead him, in the end, to greatness.

He came from Aix-en-Provence, the son of a self-made businessman who graduated from money-lending to banking, a demanding, over-bearing parent whom Cézanne respected and dreaded all his life. He expected his son to make his way in the new-rich world of the bourgeoisie, preferably as a lawyer, but eventually agreed to let him try his hand at being a painter. Cézanne came to Paris and conscientiously attended life classes at the Académie Suisse, at the same time acquaint-

Plate 56
Paul Cézanne (1839–1906)
Self-portrait
about 1875
pencil
5¾ × 4¾ in (15 × 12 cm)
The Norton Simon Foundation, Los Angeles

In his sketchbooks, as in his paintings, Cézanne explored the treatment of form. The secret of drawing and modelling, he said, lies in 'the contrasts and connections of tones'. His totally unacademic manner and procedure gave rise to the notion that Cézanne 'couldn't draw'. On the contrary, he is today numbered among the master-draughtsmen. His self-portraits in pencil are as penetrating as any he made in oils.

Plate 57
Paul Cézanne (1839–1906)
A modern Olympia
1872–73, oil on canvas
18 × 21 in (46 × 55 cm)
Louvre, Paris

Cézanne provoked bitter hostility with this painting when it was shown at the first Impressionist exhibition. Based on Manet's already legendary *Olympia*, it was probably not intended to be taken too seriously, but its sophisticated eroticism and apparent carelessness of execution were taken as a public insult. The stylishly dressed *voyeur* might be an ironic self-portrait.

ing himself with the masters in the Louvre. He was neither fluent nor easily satisfied, and his frustrations drove him to outbursts of passion which disconcerted his friends. Of these Emile Zola, who had known him from their schooldays, predicted that, though Cézanne might have the makings of a great painter, 'he will never have the genius to become one. The least obstacle makes him despair.'

Cézanne's brooding nature, fearsome appearance and coarse language combined to set a distance between him and other men, even those who felt nothing but respect for him. Though he worked closely with the Impressionists for some five years, and especially with Pissarro, he never acquired their dexterity. This was due in equal

parts to his own views on painting, which diverged from theirs at several points, and to his method of work, which was as slow and tortured as theirs was deft and vivacious. Rilke, the German poet, has left a vivid pen-picture describing how Cézanne 'gave himself entirely, his whole strength behind each stroke of the brush. You only needed to see him at work, painfully tense, his face as if in prayer, to realise how much spirit went into the task. He would shake all over, his face heavy with unseen thoughts, his chest sunken, his shoulders hunched, his hands trembling until the moment came. Then, firm and fast, they began to work gently, always from right to left, with a will of their own.'

Plate 58
Paul Cézanne (1839–1906)
The House of the Hanged Man
1872–73, oil on canvas, 21 × 26¼ in (55 × 66 cm)
Louvre, Paris

In this, his other exhibit in the 1874 Impressionist exhibition, Cézanne reveals his concern for solidity and mass while still owing much to Pissarro, his frequent companion during this period. The satisfying dignity of the *Maison du Pendu* was lost on the critics, but it did find a buyer: Count Doria, who subsequently exchanged it with the customs official Victor Chocquet.

Plate 59
Paul Cézanne (1839–1906)
Portrait of Victor Chocquet
1876–77
oil on canvas
18 × 14 in (45 × 35 cm)
Private collection

Victor Chocquet's enthusiasm for the Impressionists, and his courage in buying their works at a time when they had virtually no reputation, has ensured for him a place among the great collectors. He was a customs official, living in modest circumstances, when he first began to buy from Renoir, Manet, Monet, Sisley and, most importantly, Cézanne, for whom he had a special regard. This portrait was exhibited at the 1877 Impressionist exhibition, which Chocquet attended daily to dispute with scoffing visitors on the merits of the Impressionists' work.

Plate 60
Paul Cézanne (1839–1906)
The turning road
1879–82
oil on canvas
$23\frac{1}{2} \times 28\frac{3}{4}$ in (60 × 73 cm)
Museum of Fine Arts, Boston

Cézanne painted several landscapes in which a bending road lends force and rhythm to the structure. His aims went beyond those of the Impressionists, and his method, unlike theirs, was slow and laborious. An unusually perceptive critic, Georges Rivière, wrote in 1876: 'In all his paintings he produces emotion, because he himself experiences violent emotion which his craftsmanship then transfers to the canvas.'

Cézanne himself, when he was nearly seventy, wrote to the painter Emile Bernard: 'The main line to follow is just to put down what you see. Never mind your temperament or your ability in respect of Nature . . . Those outlines done in black are quite mistaken. The answer lies in consulting nature; that is where we find the means.' On the face of it, those are Impressionist sentiments. But Cézanne was not a man to identify himself with any particular school or set of rules. He interpreted the lessons taught him by Pissarro ('the humble and colossal Pissarro' as he called him) in his own way. Colour could produce form, but form must be more than one-dimensional. Short brushstrokes could bring life to inanimate objects, but short brushstrokes applied in parallel diagonals could bring rhythm and unity. Colours laid side by side could achieve brilliant, vibrating tones, but colours in which one plane falls on top of another contribute solidity and structure. In Cézanne's work, colour does not dissolve shapes, it gives them weight and form. The consideration given to each touch was agonising; and between each one he would carefully clean his brush. All this gives Cézanne's paintings a monumental, deep-rooted quality which harks back to the greatest masters, dismissing the accretions of centuries and stripping the painter's art to its essentials.

Cézanne's purposes were as severe as his methods. In his exploration of the painter's true function he confined himself, in the twenty years of his full maturity, to relatively simple images. He distrusted the element of decoration which he saw in the Impressionists, and was totally disinterested in the sort of subjects which delighted them: the gaiety and humanity of everyday life. His dictum 'Just put down what you see' meant something different to him, since he put his eyes to different use. He was looking for the form which underlies natural objects, and he even called his paintings 'constructions after nature'. To see things as they really are he sought to divest them of all literary and sentimental associations. He was as incapable of introducing an element of ingratiation into a picture as into a personal relationship.

The lack of such easy communication makes his work less 'popular' than that of the Impressionists, but he foresaw that this would be so. After exhibiting with the Impressionists again in 1877 he withdrew to Aix, and all but vanished from the metropolitan scene. Renoir and Monet sometimes visited him and brought back stories of the self-inflicted rigours of his life and work. In 1886 Cézanne came into his inheritance when his father died (he and his two sisters shared a fortune of two million francs) but it seemed to mean nothing to him. He continued to tramp the fields looking for subjects, destroying uncounted paintings and sketches in sudden rages, or discarding them among rocks, frightening off visitors, alternating between excitement and despair. There was, though, another side to his nature, described by Mary Cassatt: 'In spite of the total disregard of the dictionary of manners, he shows a politeness towards us which no other man here would have shown. He will not allow Louise to serve him before us in the

Plate 61
Paul Cézanne (1839–1906)
Sea at L'Estaque
1876
oil on canvas
$16\frac{1}{2} \times 23\frac{1}{4}$ in (42 × 59 cm)
The Bernhard Foundation, Inc., New York

The Impressionist period of Cézanne's development lasted five years, from 1872 to 1877, when
he was living at Auvers-sur-Oise. On the visit
to Marseilles where he painted this picture he
wrote to Pissarro: 'It is like a playing card, red
roofs on a blue sea. The sun is so fierce that
objects rise up in outline, not just black and white
but blue, red, brown and violet . . .' Cézanne's
achievement was to give a structural dimension
to light itself.

usual order of succession at the table; he is even deferential to that stupid maid, and pulls off his old tam-o'shanter, which he wears to protect his bald head, when he enters the room . . .'

In 1895 the dealer Ambroise Vollard, encouraged by Pissarro, for whom Cézanne assumed the stature of a master, decided to hold a retrospective exhibition of his works in Paris. Nobody at the time seemed to know where Cézanne was living. Vollard tracked him down, though with difficulty, and Cézanne obligingly sent him 150 rolled-up canvases. When the exhibition opened in November it made a powerful impact, not so much on the public as on the leading painters of the day. Pissarro wrote to his son Lucien: 'My enthusiasm is nothing compared with Renoir's. Even Degas has succumbed to the charm of this refined savage. Monet, all of us – were we wrong? I don't believe so . . .' There was a stirring of interest among collectors. One of Cézanne's old friends, now a senator, even put him up for the Legion of Honour: in vain. For any hint of official recognition he had to wait until 1900, when three of his works were chosen for the Century of French Art exhibition held at the Petit Palais as part of the *Exposition Internationale*. Slowly his pictures began to find buyers. When Chocquet the customs official died, his widow put seven of his Cézannes up for sale. They fetched 17,600 francs. At last his work was to be seen in exhibitions: the Salon des Indépendants, the Salon d'Automne, the Salon de la Libre Esthétique in Brussels.

On 15th October, 1906, he was caught in a shower while out painting. They carried him home, unconscious, on a washer-woman's handcart. Seven days later he died.

Plate 62
Paul Cézanne (1839–1906)
Bathers
1898–1905
oil on canvas
82 × 98½ in (208 × 249 cm)
Museum of Art, Philadelphia (Wistach Collection)

Manet's *Déjeuner sur l'herbe* remained with Cézanne as the source of his studies of nudes in a landscape painted after 1895. The series of bathers stands as one of his most important achievements, culminating in this, the largest of them (it is over eight feet wide), which he worked on during the last years of his life. His aim was to integrate human figures into a landscape, abstracting the forms and uniting them with rhythm and colour. The composition was too large to be painted from nature, as Cézanne originally visualised, and instead was built up from references to earlier masters and from his own sketchbooks. Cézanne's later work had a profound effect on the following generation of artists, notably Picasso, whose *Demoiselles d'Avignon* in 1907 heralded the birth of Cubism.

Vincent van Gogh

The term 'Post-Impressionist' was applied to Cézanne in his later years, and to two younger contemporaries, Vincent van Gogh and Paul Gauguin, in theirs.

Van Gogh entered the world of the Impressionists in 1886, when he was thirty-six. Behind him lay the experiences of an artist struggling for expression: first in Paris, then England, then back in Holland to study for the Church, followed by missionary work among the coalminers of the Borinage district of Belgium. Dismissed from the mission for 'excess of zeal' (he went about in home-made clothes, slept on the ground in a wooden hut, and gave all he had to the local poor), he wandered from Brussels to The Hague and from The Hague to Antwerp, teaching himself to paint and draw. In 1886 he joined his brother Theo, who ran an art gallery in Paris devoted to living artists, and it was there that he discovered the Impressionists.

Until then, Van Gogh had known only the Dutch painters and a handful of French landscape painters including Millet and the Barbizon group. Now, for the first time, he saw works by Delacroix (whom he later said had more effect on him than the Impressionists) and by Pissarro, Cézanne, Renoir and Sisley. Light, colour and brilliance burst upon him. He went about the streets and cafés with a palette of bright colours, as delighted by the cosmopolitan bustle of the city as Manet, Monet, Renoir and the others had been twenty years before. He met Pissarro, who was then moving towards the pointillist technique of Seurat (plate 65), a painter who excited Van Gogh, perhaps, more than any of his contemporaries at this time. It was Pissarro who uttered the famous dictum that, the moment he laid eyes on Van Gogh, 'I knew he would either go mad or surpass us all. But I did not know he would do both.'

In Antwerp, Van Gogh had not even known who the Impressionists were. Now he wrote in a letter to the English painter, Henry Livens, 'I have seen them, and though not being one of their club yet I have much admired certain Impressionist pictures – Degas' nude figures, a Claude Monet landscape'. Through the young Toulouse-Lautrec he was brought in touch with members of the avant-garde of the art world, and with the café society where Lautrec felt most at home. Van Gogh succumbed to the pleasures of an artist's life in Paris. He wrote to his sister: 'I still go on having the most impossible,

Plate 63
Vincent van Gogh (1853–90)
Moulin de la Galette, Montmartre
1886
oil on canvas
18 × 15 in (45 × 38 cm)
Glasgow Art Gallery

When Van Gogh came to Paris in 1886 he was thirty-three and in the toils of frustration and despair. His brother Theo, who ran an art gallery in Montmartre, took him in, and Van Gogh plunged into a round of work in the Louvre, meetings with other artists, and adventures in café society. His spirits brightened, and so, under the Impressionists' influence, did his palette. His paintings in the Montmartre district have a distinctively Impressionist freedom and lightness lacking in his work up to that time. 'He is certainly an artist,' Theo wrote, 'and if what he does now is not always beautiful it will certainly be useful to him later.' Paris, however, palled; his relations with Theo worsened. In February 1888 Van Gogh set off for Arles.

Plate 63 **Moulin de la Galette, Montmartre** *see page 87*

and not very seemly, love affairs from which I emerge as a rule damaged and shamed and little else.' Perhaps the woman at the 'Tambourin' was one of those who momentarily became part of his life: Toulouse-Lautrec painted her, too, in an identical pose, as *Poudre-de-riz* ('Face powder'). Another discovery was Japanese art, then at the height of its popularity. The Impressionists were enthusiastic for Japanese prints, printed in clear flat colours akin to their own ideas of colour and design. Van Gogh pinned them on his walls, and they appear in the backgrounds of some of his paintings.

This combination of influences, and the stimulus of sympathetic friends, for a time gave him new hope. But it was not long before Van Gogh grew tired of Paris. The strain of city life exhausted and depressed him, and he yearned for the sun. Toulouse-Lautrec recommended Provence. One evening, as if on an impulse, Van Gogh

Plate 64
Vincent van Gogh (1853–90)
Fishing in spring
1886–87
oil on canvas
$19\frac{1}{4} \times 22\frac{3}{4}$ in (49 × 58 cm)
Art Institute of Chicago (Gift of Charles Deering McCormick, Brooks McCormick and Roger McCormick)

Van Gogh brings to this typically Impressionist subject the vigour and definition which mark his own attitude to painting. For him, the feeling for reality was more important than the feeling for mere painting. According to his close friend at this time, the painter Emile Bernard, Van Gogh would bring back from his walks around Paris 'fragments lifted with the end of his brush and stolen, as it were, from the fleeting hour'.

Plate 65
Georges Seurat (1859–91)
Bridge at Courbevoie
1886–87
oil on canvas
18 × 21½ in (46 × 55 cm)
Courtauld Institute Galleries, London

Seurat made an appearance at the last Impressionist exhibition with a painting in the new pointillist technique. Paul Signac, his close friend and disciple, called it 'a precise and scientific method' of painting, making use of the latest theories of the nature of light. According to these, local colour, and the colour which an object assumes from the light, react on each other. The painter, by choosing and organising the elements of his picture, applying little dots of colour in accordance with these principles, could achieve realism based on scientific phenomena as well as on observation. In the *Bridge at Courbevoie* the verticals of the chimney and masts contribute an additional element of strong design.

decided to leave; but not before preparing the studio so that his brother Theo would think he was still there. He put a canvas on the easel, and piled other paintings around the walls. Then he left for Arles in the south of France, and the splendours and miseries waiting for him there.

Between February 1888 and his death by suicide eighteen months later, Van Gogh painted his greatest pictures, an achievement which, for concentrated genius, has no parallel in the history of art. Drawing on his accumulated knowledge and experience, he at once entered into his own world. By setting certain colours side by side he achieved effects of unearthly, ringing splendour. To colour he brought dignity and form, the opposite of the abstractions into which Monet was heading and which seemed the inevitable limit of Impressionist techniques. 'I am so intrigued by what really exists,' Van Gogh wrote, 'that I have neither the desire nor the courage to seek after the ideal as it might result from abstract studies.' If Van Gogh's short exposure to Impressionism at a critical moment in his life were its only claim to be remembered, it would be enough. It helped to make his art possible, no less than Cézanne's or that of the third avant-garde genius of the age, Paul Gauguin.

Paul Gauguin

Gauguin's arrival on the scene could hardly have been better timed. Impressionism, having to all appearances led nowhere in particular, was threatened by an increasing appetite in intellectual and literary circles for theosophical notions of the one-ness of art, life and sensations, and the search for metaphors in which these ideas could be expressed. The Impressionists' demonstration that truth can be captured in a glance began to look insubstantial, even if their paintings were by now beginning to be understood and, increasingly, enjoyed. Gauguin was both steeped in the Impressionists (he had his own collection of their works) and resistant to the idea that what matters in art is the sensation activated by the painter's eye. For him, as for Cézanne, the painter's function went deeper, into what he called 'the mysterious centre of the mind'.

The story of his life has become a fable, and hardly needs re-telling. After twelve years of marriage and well-paid servitude in a stockbroker's office, he abandoned his wife, children and career to become a full-time painter. He was drawn particularly to Pissarro, with whom he went painting in Pontoise, which led to his exhibiting in the Impressionist exhibitions of 1880, 1882 and 1886. Then came his move to Pont-Aven in Brittany, where he became the focus of a movement dedicated to non-naturalistic and symbolic art, its subjects drawn from dreams and fantasy. He started to paint in flat, broad areas of colour. 'Work madly and freely,' he told his group, 'and you will make progress. Above all, don't labour over your picture. A great emotion can be translated immediately. Dream over it, and look for the simplest form.' These ideas and methods were further developed in his well-known Tahitian paintings which marked the end of his Impressionist years.

The themes, colours and constructions of Gauguin's later work, by which he is best known, tend to overshadow the Impressionistic borrowings of his work in the 1880s. By then most of the group were moving away from the early innocence of the Impressionist vision. Monet's style had assumed a roughness of structure and technique; Degas was engrossed in his pastels of women at their private rituals (he never exhibited publicly after 1886); Renoir was showing a renewed concern for detail and a less mellifluous pigment; Cézanne was working out his notions of weight and form. If Gauguin looked

Plate 66
Paul Gauguin (1848–1903)
The white horse
1898
oil on canvas
55½ × 36 in (141 × 91 cm)
Louvre, Paris

His meeting with the Impressionists in 1875 changed Gauguin's life, leading him to abandon his family and career as a stockbroker to become a dedicated painter. He was closest to Pissarro and to Cézanne–'that misunderstood man,' as he called him, 'whose nature is essentially mystical and oriental'. Gauguin's own sense of mysticism produced work of startling power and ringing colour. *The white horse* is a masterly demonstration of the 'violent harmonies' which he sensed in Tahiti. A year before he died he wrote: 'If my works do not survive there will remain the memory of an artist who liberated painting from many of its former academic defects–and from its symbolist defects, which are another form of sentimentality.'

back to the beginnings of the revolution, it was to Manet's *Olympia*, which he copied in 1891. To him, and to Van Gogh, it was time to move on.

Gauguin disliked suggestions that Cézanne and Van Gogh were the effectual leaders of the Post-Impressionist movement, or that his own style owed a debt either to them or to his immediate predecessors. Nevertheless, it is a fact that he emerged at a time when the struggle to establish new principles and a new aesthetic in painting was beginning to show results, a struggle in which the Impressionists bore the brunt. Gauguin died in May 1903, on the island of his idyllic exile. In October of that year a vivid, and still valid, summary of his achievement appeared in the review *L'Orient*, written by the painter Maurice Denis. Gauguin, Denis wrote, was 'the unquestioned master who won our admiration by his talent, his fluency, his gestures, his physical strength, his harshness, his inexhaustible imagination, his very strong head for drink, his romantic bearing . . . He wanted to convey character, to express the "inner idea" even in what was ugly. He was still an Impressionist, but he sought to read the book "in which the eternal laws of Beauty are written" . . .

'But the Impressionist idea was by no means obsolete. We could subsist on what we had learnt from Renoir or Degas. Gauguin transmitted their lessons to us, enriched what he had himself borrowed from the classical tradition and from Cézanne. He revealed Cézanne's achievement to us, not as that of an independent genius, an irregular follower of Manet, but as what it really is: the end product of long exertion, the necessary result of a great crisis.'

Impressionism in Gauguin still meant sunshine, diffused light, freedom of composition, the sense of values revealed by Corot, a shimmering technique, the love of bright colour, and the influence of Japanese art. Gauguin gave artists 'the right to lyricism', to exaggerate those impressions which justify the metaphors of poetry.

Here can be seen the outline and justification for the art which was to follow, in which intuitive and subconscious responses to themes, shapes and forms were to give painters total emancipation even from their traditional materials. Cézanne, Gauguin and Van Gogh in their different ways carried Western painting into the twentieth century: Cézanne by insisting on the conceptual value of things seen, rather than simply on what strikes the eye; Gauguin by releasing the power of primitive images and symbols; and Van Gogh by the revelation of colour as a means of expressing the most intense responses of the human spirit. No doubt, in the sum of things, these were to prove more substantial even than the achievements of the Impressionists, if only because most great truths cannot be captured in a glance, however brilliantly perceptive. Even so, Impressionism marks a turning point in the history of Western art. It is still with us, still capable of invoking beauty and surprise, still communicating its unique blend of poignancy and pleasure.

Plate 66 **The white horse**

Acknowledgments

Acknowledgments for references and quotations are due to Jean Renoir, author of *Renoir, My Father*, and to the publishers of the English language edition, William Collins & Sons Ltd, England and Little, Brown & Co. Inc., USA, 1962. Other works which have provided particularly useful references include John Rewald's *The History of Impressionism*, published by the Museum of Modern Art, New York, and in England by Martin Secker & Warburg Ltd, 1973; and *Studies in Early Impressionism* by Kermit Swiler Champa, Yale University Press, 1973.

The publishers wish to express their gratitude to all those who have allowed items in their collections to be illustrated in this book and to those who have supplied photographs.

Sources of photographs
(The numbers refer to the pages on which they are reproduced)
Art Institute of Chicago 27, 55, 89; Joachim Blauel, Munich 4; Fogg Art Museum, Cambridge, Massachusetts 32 bottom, 40; Photographie Giraudon, Paris 6, 20, 32 top, 39, 42, 46–47, 56, 58, 65, 69, 80; Glasgow Art Gallery 76, 88; Hamlyn Group Picture Library 11, 14, 16, 19, 22, 23, 29, 30, 41, 45 top, 50, 62, 74 bottom, 82 top, 90; Hamlyn Group–Eric Pollitzer 49; Hamlyn Group–Tom Scott 24–25; Hamlyn Group–Studio Lourmel (Ziolo) 45 bottom; Hamlyn Group–John Webb 35, 44, 72; Metropolitan Museum of Art, New York 34; Museum of Fine Arts, Boston, Massachusetts 82 bottom; Museum of Modern Art, New York 75; National Gallery, London 37 top, 64; National Gallery of Art, Washington D.C. 8, 52–53, 54, 77; Nationalgalerie, Berlin 38; Nationalmuseum, Stockholm 60–61; Norton Simon Foundation, Los Angeles, California 78; Philadelphia Museum of Art, Pennsylvania 15, 86; La Réunion des Musées Nationaux, Paris 2, 9, 37 bottom, 48, 66, 68–69, 74 top, 93; Rheinisches Bildarchiv, Cologne 70; Scala, Antella 13; Shelburne Museum, Vermont 17; Wildenstein & Co., New York 84; Ziolo, Paris 81.

Index